THE CHILDREN OF ODIN

The Book of Northern Myths

by

PADRAIC COLUM

illustrated by
Willy Pogany

Macmillan Publishing Company
New York
Collier Macmillan Publishers
London

Macmillan Publishing Company
866 Third Avenue, New York, N.Y. 10022
Collier Macmillan Canada, Inc.

First published 1920; reissued 1984

Printed in the United States of America

10   9   8   7   6   5   4   3   2   1

Library of Congress Cataloging in Publication Data
Colum, Padraic, 1881–1972.
    The children of Odin.
    Summary: A retelling of the Norse sagas about Odin,
Freya, Thor, Loki and the other gods and goddesses who
lived in Asgard before the dawn of history.
    1. Mythology, Norse—Juvenile literature.   [1. Mythol-
ogy, Norse]   I. Pogány, Willy, 1882–1955, ill.   II. Title.
BL860.C63   1984   293'.13   83-20367
ISBN 0-02-722890-8

CONTENTS

CONTENTS

CONTENTS

PART I
THE DWELLERS
IN ASGARD

FAR AWAY AND LONG AGO

ONCE there was another Sun and another Moon; a different Sun and a different Moon from the ones we see now. Sol was the name of that Sun and Mani was the name of that Moon. But always behind Sol and Mani wolves went, a wolf behind each. The wolves caught on them at last and they devoured Sol and Mani. And then the world was in darkness and cold.

In those times the Gods lived, Odin and Thor, Hödur and Baldur, Tyr and Heimdall, Vidar and Vali, as well as Loki, the doer of good and the doer of evil. And the beautiful Goddesses were living then, Frigga, Freya, Nanna, Iduna, and Sif. But in the days when the Sun and Moon were destroyed the Gods were destroyed too — all the Gods except Baldur who had died before that time, Vidar and Vali, the sons of Odin, and Modi and Magni, the sons of Thor.

· 3 ·

At that time, too, there were men and women in the world. But before the Sun and the Moon were devoured and before the Gods were destroyed, terrible things happened in the world. Snow fell on the four corners of the earth and kept on falling for three seasons. Winds came and blew everything away. And the people of the world who had lived on in spite of the snow and the cold and the winds fought each other, brother killing brother, until all the people were destroyed.

Also there was another earth at that time, an earth green and beautiful. But the terrible winds that blew leveled down forests and hills and dwellings. Then fire came and burnt the earth. There was darkness, for the Sun and the Moon were devoured. The Gods had met with their doom. And the time in which all these things happened was called Ragnarök, the Twilight of the Gods.

Then a new Sun and a new Moon appeared and went traveling through the heavens; they were more lovely than Sol and Mani, and no wolves followed behind them in chase. The earth became green and beautiful again, and in a deep forest that the fire had not burnt a woman and a man wakened up. They had been hidden there by Odin and left to sleep during Ragnarök, the Twilight of the Gods.

Lif was the woman's name, and Lifthrasir was the man's. They moved through the world, and their children and their children's children made people for the new earth. And of the Gods were left Vidar and Vali, the sons of Odin, and Modi and Magni, the sons of Thor; on the new earth Vidar and Vali found tablets that the older Gods had written on and had left there for them, tablets telling of all that had happened before Ragnarök, the Twilight of the Gods.

And the people who lived after Ragnarök, the Twilight of the Gods, were not troubled, as the people in the older days were troubled, by the terrible beings who had brought destruction upon the world and upon men and women, and who from the beginning had waged war upon the Gods.

THE BUILDING OF THE WALL

ALWAYS there had been war between the Giants and the Gods — between the Giants who would have destroyed the world and the race of men, and the Gods who would have protected the race of men and would have made the world more beautiful.

There are many stories to be told about the Gods, but the first one that should be told to you is the one about the building of their City.

The Gods had made their way up to the top of a high mountain and there they decided to build a great City for themselves that the Giants could never overthrow. The City they would call "Asgard," which means the Place of the Gods. They would build it on a beautiful plain that was on the top of that high mountain. And they wanted to

ing it. But one who was in the company of the Gods spoke. He was Loki, a being who only half belonged to the Gods; his father was the Wind Giant. "Let the Stranger build the wall round Asgard," Loki said, "and I will find a way to make him give up the hard bargain he has made with the Gods. Go to him and tell him that the wall must be finished by the first day of Summer, and that if it is not finished to the last stone on that day the price he asks will not be given to him."

The Gods went to the Stranger and they told him that if the last stone was not laid on the wall on the first day of the Summer not Sol or Mani, the Sun and the Moon, nor Freya would be given him. And now they knew that the Stranger was one of the Giants.

The Giant and his great horse piled up the wall more quickly than before. At night, while the Giant slept, the horse worked on and on, hauling up stones and laying them on the wall with his great forefeet. And day by day the wall around Asgard grew higher and higher.

But the Gods had no joy in seeing that great wall rising higher and higher around their palaces. The Giant and his horse would finish the work by the first day of Summer, and then he would take the Sun and the Moon, Sol and Mani, and Freya away with him.

But Loki was not disturbed. He kept telling the Gods that he would find a way to prevent him from finishing his work, and thus he would make the Giant forfeit the terrible price he had led Odin to promise him.

It was three days to Summer time. All the wall was

finished except the gateway. Over the gateway a stone was still to be placed. And the Giant, before he went to sleep, bade his horse haul up a great block of stone so that they might put it above the gateway in the morning, and so finish the work two full days before Summer.

It happened to be a beautiful moonlit night. Svadilfare, the Giant's great horse, was hauling the largest stone he ever hauled when he saw a little mare come galloping toward him. The great horse had never seen so pretty a little mare and he looked at her with surprise.

"Svadilfare, slave," said the little mare to him and went frisking past.

Svadilfare put down the stone he was hauling and called to the little mare. She came back to him. "Why do you call me 'Svadilfare, slave'?" said the great horse.

"Because you have to work night and day for your master," said the little mare. "He keeps you working, working, working, and never lets you enjoy yourself. You dare not leave that stone down and come and play with me."

"Who told you I dare not do it?" said Svadilfare.

"I know you daren't do it," said the little mare, and she kicked up her heels and ran across the moonlit meadow.

Now the truth is that Svadilfare was tired of working day and night. When he saw the little mare go galloping off he became suddenly discontented. He left the stone he was hauling on the ground. He looked round and he saw the little mare looking back at him. He galloped after her.

He did not catch up on the little mare. She went on swiftly before him. On she went over the moonlit meadow,

turning and looking back now and again at the great
Svadilfare, who came heavily after her. Down the mountainside the mare went, and Svadilfare, who now rejoiced
in his liberty and in the freshness of the wind and in the
smell of the flowers, still followed her. With the morning's
light they came near a cave and the little mare went into
it. They went through the cave. Then Svadilfare caught
up on the little mare and the two went wandering together, the little mare telling Svadilfare stories of the
Dwarfs and the Elves.

They came to a grove and they stayed together in it, the
little mare playing so nicely with him that the great horse
forgot all about time passing. And while they were in the
grove the Giant was going up and down, searching for his
great horse.

He had come to the wall in the morning, expecting to
put the stone over the gateway and so finish his work. But
the stone that was to be lifted up was not near him. He
called for Svadilfare, but his great horse did not come. He
went to search for him, and he searched all down the
mountainside and he searched as far across the earth as the
realm of the Giants. But he did not find Svadilfare.

The Gods saw the first day of Summer come and the
gateway of the wall stand unfinished. They said to each
other that if it were not finished by the evening they need
not give Sol and Mani to the Giant, nor the maiden Freya
to be his wife. The hours of the summer day went past and
the Giant did not raise the stone over the gateway. In the
evening he came before them.

"Your work is not finished," Odin said. "You forced us

to a hard bargain and now we need not keep it with you. You shall not be given Sol and Mani nor the maiden Freya."

"Only the wall I have built is so strong I would tear it down," said the Giant. He tried to throw down one of the palaces, but the Gods laid hands on him and thrust him outside the wall he had built. "Go, and trouble Asgard no more," Odin commanded.

Then Loki returned to Asgard. He told the Gods how he had transformed himself into a little mare and had led away Svadilfare, the Giant's great horse. And the Gods sat in their golden palaces behind the great wall and rejoiced that their City was now secure, and that no enemy could ever enter it or overthrow it. But Odin, the Father of the Gods, as he sat upon his throne was sad in his heart, sad that the Gods had got their wall built by a trick; that oaths had been broken, and that a blow had been struck in injustice in Asgard.

IDUNA AND HER APPLES: HOW LOKI PUT THE GODS IN DANGER

IN Asgard there was a garden, and in that garden there grew a tree, and on that tree there grew shining apples. Thou knowst, O well-loved one, that every day that passes makes us older and brings us to that day when we will be bent and feeble, gray-headed and weak-eyed. But those shining apples that grew in Asgard — they who ate of them every day grew never a day older, for the eating of the apples kept old age away.

Iduna, the Goddess, tended the tree on which the shining apples grew. None would grow on the tree unless she was there to tend it. No one but Iduna might pluck the shining apples. Each morning she plucked them and left them in her basket and every day the Gods and Goddesses came to her garden that they might eat the shining apples and so stay for ever young.

Iduna never went from her garden. All day and every day she stayed in the garden or in her golden house beside it, and all day and every day she listened to Bragi, her husband, tell a story that never had an end. Ah, but a time came when Iduna and her apples were lost to Asgard, and the Gods and Goddesses felt old age approach them. How all that happened shall be told thee, O well beloved.

Odin, the Father of the Gods, often went into the land of men to watch over their doings. Once he took Loki with him, Loki, the doer of good and the doer of evil. For a long time they went traveling through the world of men. At last they came near Jötunheim, the realm of the Giants.

It was a bleak and empty region. There were no growing things there, not even trees with berries. There were no birds, there were no animals. As Odin, the Father of the Gods, and Loki, the doer of good and the doer of evil, went through this region hunger came upon them. But in all the land around they saw nothing that they could eat.

Loki, running here and running there, came at last upon a herd of wild cattle. Creeping up on them, he caught hold of a young bull and killed him. Then he cut up the flesh into strips of meat. He lighted a fire and put the meat on spits to roast. While the meat was being cooked, Odin, the Father of the Gods, a little way off, sat thinking on the things he had seen in the world of men.

Loki made himself busy putting more and more logs on the fire. At last he called to Odin, and the Father of the Gods came and sat down near the fire to eat the meal.

But when the meat was taken off the cooking-spits and when Odin went to cut it, he found that it was still raw. He smiled at Loki for thinking the meat was cooked, and Loki, troubled that he had made a mistake, put the meat back, and put more logs upon the fire. Again Loki took the meat off the cooking-spits and called Odin to the meal.

Odin, when he took the meat that Loki brought him, found that it was as raw as if it had never been put upon the fire. "Is this a trick of yours, Loki?" he said.

Loki was so angry at the meat being uncooked that Odin saw he was playing no tricks. In his hunger he raged at the meat and he raged at the fire. Again he put the meat on the cooking-spits and put more logs on the fire. Every hour he would take up the meat, sure that it was now cooked, and every time he took it off Odin would find that the meat was as raw as the first time they took it off the fire.

Now Odin knew that the meat must be under some enchantment by the Giants. He stood up and went on his way, hungry but strong. Loki, however, would not leave the meat that he had put back on the fire. He would make it be cooked, he declared, and he would not leave that place hungry.

The dawn came and he took up the meat again. As he

was lifting it off the fire he heard a whirr of wings above his head. Looking up, he saw a mighty eagle, the largest eagle that ever appeared in the sky. The eagle circled round and round and came above Loki's head. "Canst thou not cook thy food?" the eagle screamed to him.

"I cannot cook it," said Loki.

"I will cook it for thee, if thou wilt give me a share," screamed the eagle.

"Come, then, and cook it for me," said Loki.

The eagle circled round until he was above the fire. Then flapping his great wings over it, he made the fire blaze and blaze. A heat that Loki had never felt before came from the burning logs. In a minute he drew the meat from the spits and found it was well cooked.

"My share, my share, give me my share," the eagle screamed at him. He flew down, and seizing on a large piece of meat instantly devoured it. He seized on another piece. Piece after piece he devoured until it looked as if Loki would be left with no meat for his meal.

As the eagle seized on the last piece Loki became angry indeed. Taking up the spit on which the meat had been cooked, he struck at the eagle. There was a clang as if he had struck some metal. The wood of the spit did not come away. It stuck to the breast of the eagle. But Loki did not let go his hold on the spit. Suddenly the eagle rose up in the air. Loki, who held to the spit that was fastened to the eagle's breast, was drawn up with him.

Before he knew what had happened Loki was miles and miles up in the air and the eagle was flying with him toward Jötunheim, the Realm of the Giants. And the eagle was screaming out, "Loki, friend Loki, I have thee at last. It was thou who didst cheat my brother of his reward for building the wall round Asgard. But, Loki, I have thee at last. Know now that Thiassi the Giant has captured thee, O Loki, most cunning of the dwellers in Asgard."

Thus the eagle screamed as he went flying with Loki toward Jötunheim, the Realm of the Giants. They passed over the river that divides Jötunheim from Midgard, the World of Men. And now Loki saw a terrible place beneath him, a land of ice and rock. Great mountains were there: they were lighted by neither sun nor moon, but by columns of fire thrown up now and again through cracks in the earth or out of the peaks of the mountains.

Over a great iceberg the eagle hovered. Suddenly he shook the spit from his breast and Loki fell down on the ice. The eagle screamed out to him, "Thou art in my power at last, O thou most cunning of all the Dwellers in Asgard." The eagle left Loki there and flew within a crack in the mountain.

Miserable indeed was Loki upon that iceberg. The cold was deadly. He could not die there, for he was one of the Dwellers in Asgard and death might not come to him that way. He might not die, but he felt bound to that iceberg with chains of cold.

After a day his captor came to him, not as an eagle this time, but in his own form, Thiassi the Giant.

"Wouldst thou leave thine iceberg, Loki," he said, "and return to thy pleasant place in Asgard? Thou dost delight in Asgard, although only by one-half dost thou belong to the Gods. Thy father, Loki, was the Wind Giant."

"O that I might leave this iceberg," Loki said, with the tears freezing on his face.

"Thou mayst leave it when thou showest thyself ready to pay thy ransom to me," said Thiassi. "Thou wilt have to get me the shining apples that Iduna keeps in her basket."

"I cannot get Iduna's apples for thee, Thiassi," said Loki.

"Then stay upon the iceberg," said Thiassi the Giant. He went away and left Loki there with the terrible winds buffeting him as with blows of a hammer.

When Thiassi came again and spoke to him about his ransom, Loki said, "There is no way of getting the shining apples from Iduna."

"There must be some way, O cunning Loki," said the Giant.

"Iduna, although she guards well the shining apples, is simple-minded," said Loki. "It may be that I shall be able to get her to go outside the wall of Asgard. If she goes she will bring her shining apples with her, for she never lets them go out of her hand except when she gives them to the Gods and Goddesses to eat."

"Make it so that she will go beyond the wall of Asgard," said the Giant. "If she goes outside of the wall I shall get the apples from her. Swear by the World-Tree that thou wilt lure Iduna beyond the wall of Asgard. Swear it, Loki, and I shall let thee go."

"I swear it by Ygdrassil, the World-Tree, that I will lure Iduna beyond the wall of Asgard if thou wilt take me off this iceberg," said Loki.

Then Thiassi changed himself into a mighty eagle, and taking Loki in his talons, he flew with him over the stream that divides Jötunheim, the Realm of the Giants, from Midgard, the World of Men. He left Loki on the ground of Midgard, and Loki then went on his way to Asgard.

Now Odin had already returned and he had told the Dwellers in Asgard of Loki's attempt to cook the enchanted meat. All laughed to think that Loki had been left hungry for all his cunning. Then when he came into Asgard looking so famished, they thought it was because Loki had had nothing to eat. They laughed at him more and more. But they brought him into the Feast Hall and they gave him the best of food with wine out of Odin's wine cup. When the feast was over the Dwellers in Asgard went to Iduna's garden as was their wont.

There sat Iduna in the golden house that opened on her garden. Had she been in the world of men, every one who saw her would have remembered their own innocence, seeing one who was so fair and good. She had eyes blue as the blue sky, and she smiled as if she were remembering lovely things she had seen or heard. The basket of shining apples was beside her.

To each God and Goddess Iduna gave a shining apple. Each one ate the apple given, rejoicing to think that they would never become a day older. Then Odin, the Father of the Gods, said the runes that were always said in praise of Iduna, and the Dwellers in Asgard went out of Iduna's garden, each one going to his or her own shining house.

All went except Loki, the doer of good and the doer of evil. Loki sat in the garden, watching fair and simple Iduna. After a while she spoke to him and said, "Why dost thou still stay here, wise Loki?"

"To look well on thine apples," Loki said. "I am wondering if the apples I saw yesterday are really as shining as the apples that are in thy basket."

"There are no apples in the world as shining as mine," said Iduna.

"The apples I saw were more shining," said Loki. "Aye, and they smelled better, Iduna."

Iduna was troubled at what Loki, whom she deemed so wise, told her. Her eyes filled with tears that there might be more shining apples in the world than hers. "O Loki," she said, "it cannot be. No apples are more shining, and none smell so sweet, as the apples I pluck off the tree in my garden."

"Go, then, and see," said Loki. "Just outside Asgard is the tree that has the apples I saw. Thou, Iduna, dost never leave thy garden, and so thou dost not know what grows in the world. Go outside of Asgard and see."

"I will go, Loki," said Iduna, the fair and simple.

Iduna went outside the wall of Asgard. She went to the place Loki had told her that the apples grew in. But as she looked this way and that way, Iduna heard a whirr of wings above her. Looking up, she saw a mighty eagle, the largest eagle that had ever appeared in the sky.

She drew back toward the gate of Asgard. Then the great eagle swooped down; Iduna felt herself lifted up, and then she was being carried away from Asgard, away, away; away over Midgard where men lived, away toward the rocks and snows of Jötunheim. Across the river that flows between the World of Men and the Realm of the Giants Iduna was borne. Then the eagle flew into a cleft in a mountain and Iduna was left in a cavernous hall lighted up by columns of fire that burst up from the earth.

The eagle loosened his grip on Iduna and she sank down on the ground of the cavern. The wings and the feathers fell from him and she saw her captor as a terrible Giant.

"Oh, why have you carried me off from Asgard and brought me to this place?" Iduna cried.

"That I might eat your shining apples, Iduna," said Thiassi the Giant.

"That will never be, for I will not give them to you," said Iduna.

"Give me the apples to eat, and I shall carry you back to Asgard."

"No, no, that cannot be. I have been trusted with the shining apples that I might give them to the Gods only."

"Then I shall take the apples from you," said Thiassi the Giant.

He took the basket out of her hands and opened it. But when he touched the apples they shriveled under his hands. He left them in the basket and he set the basket down, for he knew now that the apples would be no good to him unless Iduna gave them to him with her own hands.

"You must stay with me here until you give me the shining apples," he said to her.

Then was poor Iduna frightened: she was frightened of the strange cave and frightened of the fire that kept bursting up out of the earth and she was frightened of the terrible Giant. But above all she was frightened to think of the evil that would fall upon the Dwellers in Asgard if she were not there to give them the shining apples to eat.

The Giant came to her again. But still Iduna would not give him the shining apples. And there in the cave she stayed, the Giant troubling her every day. And she grew more and more fearful as she saw in her dreams the Dwellers in Asgard go to her garden — go there, and not being given the shining apples, feel and see a change coming over themselves and over each other.

It was as Iduna saw it in her dreams. Every day the Dwellers in Asgard went to her garden — Odin and Thor, Hödur and Baldur, Tyr and Heimdall, Vidar and Vali, with Frigga, Freya, Nanna, and Sif. There was no one to pluck the apples of their tree. And a change began to come over the Gods and Goddesses.

They no longer walked lightly; their shoulders became bent; their eyes no longer were as bright as dewdrops. And when they looked upon one another they saw the change. Age was coming upon the Dwellers in Asgard.

They knew that the time would come when Frigga would be gray and old; when Sif's golden hair would fade; when Odin would no longer have his clear wisdom, and when Thor would not have strength enough to raise and fling his thunderbolts. And the Dwellers in Asgard were saddened by this knowledge, and it seemed to them that all brightness had gone from their shining City.

Where was Iduna whose apples would give back youth and strength and beauty to the Dwellers in Asgard? The Gods had searched for her through the World of Men. No trace of her did they find. But now Odin, searching through his wisdom, saw a means to get knowledge of where Iduna was hidden.

He summoned his two ravens, Hugin and Munin, his two ravens that flew through the earth and through the Realm of the Giants and that knew all things that were past and all things that were to come. He summoned Hugin and Munin and they came, and one sat on his right shoulder and one sat on his left shoulder and they told him deep secrets: they told him of Thiassi and of his desire for the shining apples that the Dwellers in Asgard ate, and of Loki's deception of Iduna, the fair and simple.

What Odin learnt from his ravens was told in the Council of the Gods. Then Thor the Strong went to Loki and laid hands upon him. When Loki found himself in the grip of the strong God, he said, "What wouldst thou with me, O Thor?"

"I would hurl thee into a chasm in the ground and strike thee with my thunder," said the strong God. "It was thou who didst bring it about that Iduna went from Asgard."

"O Thor," said Loki, "do not crush me with thy thun-

· 23 ·

der. Let me stay in Asgard. I will strive to win Iduna back."

"The judgment of the Gods," said Thor, "is that thou, the cunning one, shouldst go to Jötunheim, and by thy craft win Iduna back from the Giants. Go or else I shall hurl thee into a chasm and crush thee with my thunder."

"I will go," said Loki.

From Frigga, the wife of Odin, Loki borrowed the dress of falcon feathers that she owned. He clad himself in it, and flew to Jötunheim in the form of a falcon.

He searched through Jötunheim until he found Thiassi's daughter, Skadi. He flew before Skadi and he let the Giant maid catch him and hold him as a pet. One day the Giant maid carried him into the cave where Iduna, the fair and simple, was held.

When Loki saw Iduna there he knew that part of his quest was ended. Now he had to get Iduna out of Jötunheim and away to Asgard. He stayed no more with the Giant maid, but flew up into the high rocks of the cave. Skadi wept for the flight of her pet, but she ceased to search and to call and went away from the cave.

Then Loki, the doer of good and the doer of evil, flew to where Iduna was sitting and spoke to her. Iduna, when she knew that one of the Dwellers in Asgard was near, wept with joy.

Loki told her what she was to do. By the power of a spell that was given him he was able to change her into the form of a sparrow. But before she did this she took the shining apples out of her basket and flung them into places where the Giant would never find them.

Skadi, coming back to the cave, saw the falcon fly out with the sparrow beside him. She cried out to her father and the Giant knew that the falcon was Loki and the sparrow was Iduna. He changed himself into the form of a mighty eagle. By this time sparrow and falcon were out of sight, but Thiassi, knowing that he could make better flight than they, flew toward Asgard.

Soon he saw them. They flew with all the power they had, but the great wings of the eagle brought him nearer and nearer to them. The Dwellers in Asgard, standing on the wall, saw the falcon and the sparrow with the great eagle pursuing them. They knew who they were — Loki and Iduna with Thiassi in pursuit.

As they watched the eagle winging nearer and nearer, the Dwellers in Asgard were fearful that the falcon and the sparrow would be caught upon and that Iduna would be taken again by Thiassi. They lighted great fires upon the wall, knowing that Loki would find a way through the fires, bringing Iduna with him, but that Thiassi would not find a way.

The falcon and the sparrow flew toward the fires. Loki went between the flames and brought Iduna with him. And Thiassi, coming up to the fires and finding no way through, beat his wings against the flames. He fell down from the wall and the death that came to him afterwards was laid to Loki.

Thus Iduna was brought back to Asgard. Once again she sat in the golden house that opened to her garden, once again she plucked the shining apples off the tree she tended, and once again she gave them to the Dwellers in Asgard. And the Dwellers in Asgard walked lightly again, and brightness came into their eyes and into their cheeks; age no more approached them; youth came back; light and joy were again in Asgard.

SIF'S GOLDEN HAIR: HOW LOKI
WROUGHT MISCHIEF IN ASGARD

ALL who dwelt in Asgard, the Æsir and the Asyniur, who were the Gods and the Goddesses, and the Vanir, who were the friends of the Gods and the Goddesses, were wroth with Loki. It was no wonder they were wroth with him, for he had let the Giant Thiassi carry off Iduna and her golden apples. Still, it must be told that the show they made of their wrath made Loki ready to do more mischief in Asgard.

One day he saw a chance to do mischief that made his heart rejoice. Sif, the wife of Thor, was lying asleep outside her house. Her beautiful golden hair flowed all round her. Loki knew how much Thor loved that shining hair, and how greatly Sif prized it because of Thor's love. Here was his chance to do a great mischief. Smilingly, he took out his shears and he cut off the shining hair, every strand and every tress. She did not waken while her treasure was being taken from her. But Loki left Sif's head cropped and bare.

Thor was away from Asgard. Coming back to the City of the Gods, he went into his house. Sif, his wife, was not there to welcome him. He called to Sif, but no glad answer came from her. To the palaces of all the Gods and Goddesses Thor went, but in none of them did he find Sif, his golden-haired wife.

When he was coming back to his house he heard his name whispered. He stopped, and then a figure stole out from behind a stone. A veil covered her head, and Thor scarce knew that this was Sif, his wife. As he went to her she sobbed and sobbed. "O Thor, my husband," she said, "do not look upon me. I am ashamed that you should see me. I shall go from Asgard and from the company of the Gods and Goddesses, and I shall go down to Svartheim and live amongst the Dwarfs. I cannot bear that any of the Dwellers in Asgard should look upon me now."

"O Sif," cried Thor, "what has happened to change you?"

"I have lost the hair of my head," said Sif, "I have lost the beautiful golden hair that you, Thor, loved. You will not love me any more, and so I must go away, down to Svartheim and to the company of the Dwarfs. They are as ugly as I am now."

Then she took the veil off her head and Thor saw that

all her beautiful hair was gone. She stood before him, shamed and sorrowful, and he grew into a mighty rage. "Who was it did this to you, Sif?" he said. "I am Thor, the strongest of all the Dwellers in Asgard, and I shall see to it that all the powers the Gods possess will be used to get your fairness back. Come with me, Sif." And taking his wife's hand in his, Thor went off to the Council House where the Gods and the Goddesses were.

Sif covered her head with her veil, for she would not have the Gods and Goddesses look upon her shorn head. But from the anger in Thor's eyes all saw that the wrong done to Sif was great indeed. Then Thor told of the cutting of her beautiful hair. A whisper went round the Council House. "It was Loki did this — no one else in Asgard would have done a deed so shameful," one said to the other.

"Loki it was who did it," said Thor. "He has hidden himself, but I shall find him and I will slay him."

"Nay, not so, Thor," said Odin, the Father of the Gods. "Nay, no Dweller in Asgard may slay another. I shall summon Loki to come before us here. It is for you to make him (and remember that Loki is cunning and able to do many things) bring back to Sif the beauty of her golden hair."

Then the call of Odin, the call that all in Asgard have to harken to, went through the City of the Gods. Loki heard it, and he had to come from his hiding-place and enter the house where the Gods held their Council. And when he looked on Thor and saw the rage that was in his eyes, and when he looked on Odin and saw the sternness in the face of the Father of the Gods, he knew that he would have to make amends for the shameful wrong he had done to Sif.

Said Odin, "There is a thing that you, Loki, have to do: Restore to Sif the beauty of her hair."

Loki looked at Odin, Loki looked at Thor, and he saw that what was said would have to be done. His quick mind searched to find a way of restoring to Sif the beauty of her golden hair.

"I shall do as you command, Odin All-Father," he said.

But before we tell you of what Loki did to restore the beauty of Sif's golden hair, we must tell you of the other beings besides the Gods and the Goddesses who were in the world at the time. First, there was the Vanir. When the Gods who were called the Æsir came to the mountain on which they built Asgard, they found other beings there. These were not wicked and ugly like the Giants; they were beautiful and friendly; the Vanir they were named.

Although they were beautiful and friendly the Vanir had no thought of making the world more beautiful or more happy. In that way they differed from the Æsir who had such a thought. The Æsir made peace with them, and they lived together in friendship, and the Vanir came to do things that helped the Æsir to make the world more beautiful and more happy. Freya, whom the Giant wanted to take away with the Sun and the Moon as a reward for the building of the wall round Asgard, was of the Vanir.

The other beings of the Vanir were Frey, who was the brother of Freya, and Niörd, who was their father.

On the earth below there were other beings — the dainty Elves, who danced and fluttered about, attending to the trees and flowers and grasses. The Vanir were permitted to rule over the Elves. Then below the earth, in caves and hollows, there was another race, the Dwarfs or Gnomes, little, twisted creatures, who were both wicked and ugly, but who were the best craftsmen in the world.

In the days when neither the Æsir nor the Vanir were friendly to him Loki used to go down to Svartheim, the Dwarfs' dwelling below the earth. And now that he was commanded to restore to Sif the beauty of her hair, Loki thought of help he might get from the Dwarfs.

Down, down, through the winding passages in the earth he went, and he came at last to where the Dwarfs who were most friendly to him were working in their forges. All the Dwarfs were master-smiths, and when he came upon his friends he found them working hammer and tongs, beating metals into many shapes. He watched them for a while and took note of the things they were making. One was a spear, so well balanced and made that it would hit whatever mark it was thrown at no matter how bad the aim the thrower had. The other was a boat that could sail on any sea, but that could be folded up so that it would go into one's pocket. The spear was called Gungnir and the boat was called Skidbladnir.

Loki made himself very agreeable to the Dwarfs, praising their work and promising them things that only the Dwellers in Asgard could give, things that the Dwarfs longed to possess. He talked to them till the little, ugly folk thought that they would come to own Asgard and all that was in it.

At last Loki said to them, "Have you got a bar of fine gold that you can hammer into threads — into threads so fine that they will be like the hair of Sif, Thor's wife? Only the Dwarfs could make a thing so wonderful. Ah, there is the bar of gold. Hammer it into those fine threads, and the Gods themselves will be jealous of your work."

Flattered by Loki's speeches, the Dwarfs who were in the forge took up the bar of fine gold and flung it into the fire. Then taking it out and putting it upon their anvil they worked on the bar with their tiny hammers until they beat it into threads that were as fine as the hairs of one's head. But that was not enough. They had to be as fine as the hairs on Sif's head, and these were finer than anything else. They worked on the threads, over and over again, until they were as fine as the hairs on Sif's head. The threads were as bright as sunlight, and when Loki took up the mass of worked gold it flowed from his raised hand down on the ground. It was so fine that it could be put into his palm, and it was so light that a bird might not feel its weight.

Then Loki praised the Dwarfs more and more, and he made more and more promises to them. He charmed them all, although they were an unfriendly and a suspicious folk. And before he left them he asked them for the spear and the boat he had seen them make, the spear Gungnir and the boat Skidbladnir. The Dwarfs gave him these things, though in a while after they wondered at themselves for giving them.

Back to Asgard Loki went. He walked into the Council House where the Dwellers in Asgard were gathered. He met the stern look in Odin's eyes and the rageful look in Thor's eyes with smiling good humor. "Off with thy veil, O Sif," he said. And when poor Sif took off her veil he put upon her shorn head the wonderful mass of gold he held in his palm. Over her shoulders the gold fell, fine, soft, and shining as her own hair. And the Æsir and the Asyniur, the Gods and the Goddesses, and the Van and Vana, when they saw Sif's head covered again with the shining web, laughed and clapped their hands in gladness. And the shining web held to Sif's head as if indeed it had roots and was growing there.

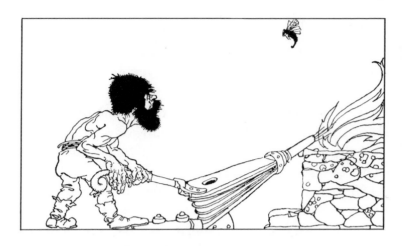

HOW BROCK BROUGHT
JUDGMENT ON LOKI

IT was then that Loki, with the wish of making the Æsir
and the Vanir friendly to him once more, brought out
the wonderful things he had gained from the Dwarfs —
the spear Gungnir and the boat Skidbladnir. The Æsir
and the Vanir marveled at things so wonderful. Loki gave
the spear as a gift to Odin, and to Frey, who was chief of
the Vanir, he gave the boat Skidbladnir.

All Asgard rejoiced that things so wonderful and so
helpful had been brought to them. And Loki, who had
made a great show in giving these gifts, said boastingly:

"None but the Dwarfs who work for me could make
such things. There are other Dwarfs, but they are as un-
handy as they are misshapen. The Dwarfs who are my

servants are the only ones who can make such wonders."

Now Loki in his boastfulness had said a foolish thing. There were other Dwarfs besides those who had worked for him, and one of these was there in Asgard. All unknown to Loki he stood in the shadow of Odin's seat, listening to what was being said. Now he went over to Loki, his little, unshapely form trembling with rage — Brock, the most spiteful of all the Dwarfs.

"Ha, Loki, you boaster," he roared, "you lie in your words. Sindri, my brother, who would scorn to serve you, is the best smith in Svartheim."

The Æsir and the Vanir laughed to see Loki outfaced by Brock the Dwarf in the middle of his boastfulness. As they laughed Loki grew angry.

"Be silent, Dwarf," he said, "your brother will know about smith's work when he goes to the Dwarfs who are my friends, and learns something from them."

"He learn from the Dwarfs who are your friends! My brother Sindri learn from the Dwarfs who are your friends!" Brock roared, in a greater rage than before. "The things you have brought out of Svartheim would not be noticed by the Æsir and the Vanir if they were put beside the things that my brother Sindri can make."

"Sometime we will try your brother Sindri and see what he can do," said Loki.

"Try now, try now," Brock shouted. "I'll wager my head against yours, Loki, that his work will make the Dwellers in Asgard laugh at your boasting."

"I will take your wager," said Loki. "My head against

yours. And glad will I be to see that ugly head of yours off your misshapen shoulders."

"The Æsir will judge whether my brother's work is not the best that ever came out of Svartheim. And they will see to it that you will pay your wager, Loki, the head off your shoulders. Will ye not sit in judgment, O Dwellers in Asgard?"

"We will sit in judgment," said the Æsir. Then, still full of rage, Brock the Dwarf went down to Svartheim, and to the place where his brother Sindri worked.

There was Sindri in his glowing forge, working with bellows and anvil and hammers beside him, and around him masses of metal — gold and silver, copper and iron. Brock told his tale, how he had wagered his head against Loki's that Sindri could make things more wonderful than the spear and the boat that Loki had brought into Asgard.

"You were right in what you said, my brother," said Sindri, "and you shall not lose your head to Loki. But the two of us must work at what I am going to forge. It will be your work to keep the fire so that it will neither blaze up nor die down for a single instant. If you can keep the fire as I tell you, we will forge a wonder. Now, brother, keep your hands upon the bellows, and keep the fire under your control."

Then into the fire Sindri threw, not a piece of metal, but a pig's skin. Brock kept his hands on the bellows, working it so that the fire neither died down nor blazed up for a single instant. And in the glowing fire the pigskin swelled itself into a strange shape.

But Brock was not left to work the bellows in peace. In

to the forge flew a gadfly. It lighted on Brock's hands and stung them. The Dwarf screamed with pain, but his hands still held the bellows, working it to keep the fire steady, for he knew that the gadfly was Loki, and that Loki was striving to spoil Sindri's work. Again the gadfly stung his hands, but Brock, although his hands felt as if they were pierced with hot irons, still worked the bellows so that the fire did not blaze up or die down for a single instant.

Sindri came and looked into the fire. Over the shape that was rising there he said words of magic. The gadfly had flown away, and Sindri bade his brother cease working. He took out the thing that had been shaped in the fire, and he worked over it with his hammer. It was a wonder indeed — a boar, all golden, that could fly through the air, and that shed light from its bristles as it flew. Brock forgot the pain in his hands and screamed with joy. "This is the greatest of wonders," he said. "The Dwellers in Asgard will have to give the judgment against Loki. I shall have Loki's head!"

But Sindri said, "The boar Golden Bristle may not be judged as great a wonder as the spear Gungnir or the boat Skidbladnir. We must make something more wonderful still. Work the bellows as before, brother, and do not let the fire die down or blaze up for a single instant."

Then Sindri took up a piece of gold that was so bright it lightened up the dark cavern that the Dwarfs worked in. He threw the piece of gold into the fire. Then he went to make ready something else and left Brock to work the bellows.

The gadfly flew in again. Brock did not know it was

there until it lighted on the back of his neck. It stung him till Brock felt the pain was wrenching him apart. But still he kept his hands on the bellows, working it so that the fire neither blazed up nor died down for a single instant. When Sindri came to look into the fire, Brock was not able to speak for pain.

Again Sindri said magic words over the gold that was being smelted in the fire. He took it out of the glow and worked it over on the main-anvil. Then in a while he showed Brock something that looked like the circle of the sun. "A splendid armring, my brother," he said. "An armring for a God's right arm. And this ring has hidden wonders. Every ninth night eight rings like itself will drop from this armring, for this is Draupnir, the Ring of Increase."

"To Odin, the Father of the Gods, the ring shall be given," said Brock. "And Odin will have to declare that nothing so wonderful or so profitable to the Gods was ever brought into Asgard. O Loki, cunning Loki, I shall have thy head in spite of thy tricks."

"Be not too hasty, brother," said Sindri. "What we have done so far is good. But better still must be the thing that will make the Dwellers in Asgard give the judgment that delivers Loki's head to thee. Work as before, brother, and do not let the fire blaze up or die down for a single instant."

This time Sindri threw into the fire a bar of iron. Then he went away to fetch the hammer that would shape it. Brock worked the bellows as before, but only his hands were steady, for every other part of him was trembling with expectation of the gadfly's sting.

He saw the gadfly dart into the forge. He screamed as it flew round and round him, searching out a place where it might sting him most fearfully. It lighted down on his forehead, just between his eyes. The first sting it gave took the sight from his eyes. It stung again and Brock felt the blood flowing down. Darkness filled the cave. Brock tried to keep his hands steady on the bellows, but he did not know whether the fire was blazing up or dying down. He shouted and Sindri hurried up.

Sindri said the magic words over the thing that was in the fire. Then he drew it out. "An instant more," he said, "and the work would have been perfect. But because you let the fire die down for an instant the work is not as good as it might have been made." He took what was shaped in the fire to the main-anvil and worked over it. Then when Brock's eyesight came back to him he saw a great hammer, a hammer all of iron. The handle did not seem to be long enough to balance the head. This was because the fire had died down for an instant while it was being formed.

"The hammer is Miölnir," said Sindri, "and it is the greatest of the things that I am able to make. All in Asgard must rejoice to see this hammer. Thor only will be able to wield it. Now I am not afraid of the judgment that the Dwellers in Asgard will give."

"The Dwellers in Asgard will have to give judgment for us," Brock cried out. "They will have to give judgment for us, and the head of Loki, my tormentor, will be given me."

"No more wonderful or more profitable gifts than these have ever been brought into Asgard," Sindri said. "Thy head is saved, and thou wilt be able to take the head of Loki who was insolent to us. Bring it here, and we will throw it into the fire in the forge."

The Æsir and the Vanir were seated in the Council House of Asgard when a train of Dwarfs appeared before them. Brock came at the head of the train, and he was followed by a band of Dwarfs carrying things of great weight. Brock and his attendants stood round the throne of Odin, and harkened to the words of the Father of the Gods.

"We know why you have come into Asgard from out of Svartheim," Odin said. "You have brought things wonderful and profitable to the Dwellers in Asgard. Let what you have brought be seen, Brock. If they are more wonderful and more useful than the things Loki has brought out of Svartheim, the spear Gungnir and the boat Skidbladnir, we will give judgment for you."

Then Brock commanded the Dwarfs who waited on him to show the Dwellers in Asgard the first of the wonders that Sindri had made. They brought out the boar, Golden Bristle. Round and round the Council House the boar flew, leaving a track of brightness. The Dwellers in Asgard said one to the other that this was a wonder indeed. But none would say that the boar was a better thing to have in Asgard than the spear that would hit the mark no matter how badly it was flung, or the boat Skidbladnir that would sail on any sea, and that could be folded up so small that it would fit in any one's pocket: none would say that Golden Bristle was better than these wonders.

To Frey, who was Chief of the Vanir, Brock gave the wondrous boar.

Then the attending Dwarfs showed the armring that was as bright as the circle of the Sun. All admired the noble ring. And when it was told how every ninth night this ring dropped eight rings of gold that were like itself, the Dwellers in Asgard spoke aloud, all saying that Draupnir, the Ring of Increase, was a wonder indeed. Hearing their voices raised, Brock looked triumphantly at Loki who was standing there with his lips drawn closely together.

To Odin, the Father of the Gods, Brock gave the noble armring.

Then he commanded the attending Dwarfs to lay before Thor the hammer Miölnir. Thor took the hammer up and swung it around his head. As he did so he uttered a great cry. And the eyes of the Dwellers in Asgard lightened up when they saw Thor with the hammer Miölnir in his hands; their eyes lightened up and from their lips came the cry, "This is a wonder, a wonder indeed! With this hammer in his hand none can withstand Thor, our Champion. No greater thing has ever come into Asgard than the hammer Miölnir."

Then Odin, the Father of the Gods, spoke from his throne, giving judgment. "The hammer Miölnir that the Dwarf Brock has brought into Asgard is a thing wonderful indeed and profitable to the Gods. In Thor's hands it can crush mountains, and hurl the Giant race from the ramparts of Asgard. Sindri the Dwarf has forged a greater thing than the spear Gungnir and the boat Skidbladnir. There can be no other judgment."

Brock looked at Loki, showing his gnarled teeth. "Now, Loki, yield your head, yield your head," he cried.

"Do not ask such a thing," said Odin. "Put any other penalty on Loki for mocking you and tormenting you. Make him yield to you the greatest thing that it is in his power to give."

"Not so, not so," screamed Brock. "You Dwellers in Asgard would shield one another. But what of me? Loki would have taken my head had I lost the wager. Loki has lost his head to me. Let him kneel down now till I cut it off."

Loki came forward, smiling with closed lips. "I kneel before you, Dwarf," he said. "Take off my head. But be careful. Do not touch my neck. I did not bargain that you should touch my neck. If you do, I shall call upon the Dwellers in Asgard to punish you."

Brock drew back with a snarl. "Is this the judgment of the Gods?" he asked.

"The bargain you made, Brock," said Odin, "was an evil one, and all its evil consequences you must bear."

Brock, in a rage, looked upon Loki, and he saw that his lips were smiling. He stamped his feet and raged. Then he went up to Loki and said, "I may not take your head, but I can do something with your lips that mock me."

"What would you do, Dwarf?" asked Thor.

"Sew Loki's lips together," said Brock, "so that he can do no more mischief with his talk. You Dwellers in Asgard cannot forbid me to do this. Down, Loki, on your knees before me."

Loki looked round on the Dwellers in Asgard and he saw that their judgment was that he must kneel before the Dwarf. He knelt down with a frown upon his brow. "Draw your lips together, Loki," said Brock. Loki drew his lips together while his eyes flashed fire. With an awl that he took from his belt Brock pierced Loki's lips. He took out a thong and tightened them together. Then in triumph the Dwarf looked on Loki.

"O Loki," he said, "you boasted that the Dwarfs who worked for you were better craftsmen than Sindri, my brother. Your words have been shown to be lies. And now you cannot boast for a while."

Then Brock the Dwarf, with great majesty, walked out of the Council House of Asgard, and the attending Dwarfs marched behind him in procession. Down the passages in the earth the Dwarfs went, singing the song of Brock's triumph over Loki. And in Svartheim it was told forever after how Sindri and Brock had prevailed.

In Asgard, now that Loki's lips were closed, there was peace and a respite from mischief. No one amongst the Æsir or the Vanir were sorry when Loki had to walk about in silence with his head bent low.

HOW FREYA GAINED HER NECKLACE AND HOW HER LOVED ONE WAS LOST TO HER

YES, Loki went through Asgard silent and with head bent, and the Dwellers in Asgard said one unto the other, "This will teach Loki to work no more mischief." They did not know that what Loki had done had sown the seeds of mischief and that these seeds were to sprout up and bring sorrow to the beautiful Vana Freya, to Freya whom the Giant wanted to carry off with the Sun and the Moon as payment for his building the wall around Asgard.

Freya had looked upon the wonders that Loki had brought into Asgard — the golden threads that were Sif's hair, and Frey's boar that shed light from its bristles as it flew. The gleam of these golden things dazzled her, and made her dream in the day time and the night time of the wonders that she herself might possess. And often she thought, "What wonderful things the Three Giant Women would give me if I could bring myself to go to them on their mountaintop."

Long ere this, when the wall around their City was not yet built, and when the Gods had set up only the court with their twelve seats and the Hall that was for Odin and the Hall that was for the Goddesses, there had come into Asgard Three Giant Women.

They came after the Gods had set up a forge and had begun to work metal for their buildings. The metal they worked was pure gold. With gold they built Gladsheim, the Hall of Odin, and with gold they made all their dishes and household ware. Then was the Age of Gold, and the Gods did not grudge gold to anyone. Happy were the Gods then, and no shadow nor foreboding lay on Asgard.

But after the Three Giant Women came the Gods began to value gold and to hoard it. They played with it no more. And the happy innocence of their first days departed from them.

At last the Three were banished from Asgard. The Gods turned their thoughts from the hoarding of gold, and they built up their City, and they made themselves strong.

And now Freya, the lovely Vanir bride, thought upon the Giant Women and on the wonderful things of gold they had flashed through their hands. But not to Odur, her husband, did she speak her thoughts; for Odur, more than any of the other dwellers in Asgard, was wont to think on the days of happy innocence, before gold came to be hoarded and valued. Odur would not have Freya go near the mountaintop where the Three had their high seat.

But Freya did not cease to think upon them and upon the things of gold they had. "Why should Odur know I went to them?" she said to herself. "No one will tell him. And what difference will it make if I go to them and gain some lovely thing for myself? I shall not love Odur the less because I go my own way for once."

Then one day she left their palace, leaving Odur, her husband, playing with their little child Hnossa. She left the palace and went down to the Earth. There she stayed for a while, tending the flowers that were her charge. After a while she asked the Elves to tell her where the mountain was on which the Three Giant Women stayed.

The Elves were frightened and would not tell her, although she was queen over them. She left them and stole down into the caves of the Dwarfs. It was they who showed her the way to the seat of the Giant Women, but before they showed her the way they made her feel shame and misery.

"We will show you the way if you stay with us here," said one of the Dwarfs.

"For how long would you have me stay?" said Freya.

"Until the cocks in Svartheim crow," said the Dwarfs, closing round her. "We want to know what the company of one of the Vanir is like." "I will stay," Freya said.

. 46 .

Then one of the Dwarfs reached up and put his arms round her neck and kissed her with his ugly mouth. Freya tried to break away from them, but the Dwarfs held her. "You cannot go away from us now until the cocks of Svartheim crow," they said.

Then one and then another of the Dwarfs pressed up to her and kissed her. They made her sit down beside them on the heaps of skins they had. When she wept they screamed at her and beat her. One, when she would not kiss him on the mouth, bit her hands. So Freya stayed with the Dwarfs until the cocks of Svartheim crew.

They showed her the mountain on the top of which the Three banished from Asgard had their abode. The Giant Women sat overlooking the World of Men. "What would you have from us, wife of Odur?" one who was called Gulveig said to her.

"Alas! Now that I have found you I know that I should ask you for nought," Freya said.

"Speak, Vana," said the second of the Giant Women.

The third said nothing, but she held up in her hands a necklace of gold most curiously fashioned. "How bright it is!" Freya said. "There is shadow where you sit, women, but the necklace you hold makes brightness now. Oh, how I should joy to wear it!"

"It is the necklace Brisingamen," said the one who was called Gulveig.

"It is yours to wear, wife of Odur," said the one who held it in her hands.

Freya took the shining necklace and clasped it round her throat. She could not bring herself to thank the Giant

Women, for she saw that there was evil in their eyes. She made reverence to them, however, and she went from the mountain on which they sat overlooking the World of Men.

In a while she looked down and saw Brisingamen and her misery went from her. It was the most beautiful thing ever made by hands. None of the Asyniur and none other of the Vanir possessed a thing so beautiful. It made her more and more lovely, and Odur, she thought, would forgive her when he saw how beautiful and how happy Brisingamen made her.

She rose up from amongst the flowers and took leave of the slight Elves and she made her way into Asgard. All who greeted her looked long and with wonder upon the necklace that she wore. And into the eyes of the Goddesses there came a look of longing when they saw Brisingamen.

But Freya hardly stopped to speak to anyone. As swiftly as she could she made her way to her own palace. She would show herself to Odur and win his forgiveness. She entered her shining palace and called to him. No answer came. Her child, the little Hnossa, was on the floor, playing. Her mother took her in her arms, but the child, when she looked on Brisingamen, turned away crying.

Freya left Hnossa down and searched again for Odur. He was not in any part of their palace. She went into the houses of all who dwelt in Asgard, asking for tidings of him. None knew where he had gone to. At last Freya went back to their palace and waited and waited for Odur to return. But Odur did not come.

One came to her. It was a Goddess, Odin's wife, the queenly Frigga. "You are waiting for Odur, your husband," Frigga said. "Ah, let me tell you Odur will not come to you here. He went, when for the sake of a shining thing you did what would make him unhappy. Odur has gone from Asgard and no one knows where to search for him."

"I will seek him outside of Asgard," Freya said. She wept no more, but she took the little child Hnossa and put her in Frigga's arms. Then she mounted her car that was drawn by two cats, and journeyed down from Asgard to Midgard, the Earth, to search for Odur her husband.

Year in and year out, and over all the Earth, Freya went searching and calling for the lost Odur. She went as far as the bounds of the Earth, where she could look over to Jötunheim, where dwelt the Giant who would have carried her off with the Sun and the Moon as payment for the building of the wall around Asgard. But in no place, from the end of the Rainbow Bifröst, that stretched from Asgard to the Earth, to the boundary of Jötunheim, did she find a trace of her husband Odur.

At last she turned her car toward Bifröst, the Rainbow Bridge that stretched from Midgard, the Earth, to Asgard, the Dwelling of the Gods. Heimdall, the Watcher for the Gods, guarded the Rainbow Bridge. To him Freya went with a half hope fluttering in her heart.

"O Heimdall," she cried, "O Heimdall, Watcher for the Gods, speak and tell me if you know where Odur is."

"Odur is in every place where the searcher has not

come; Odur is in every place that the searcher has left; those who seek him will never find Odur," said Heimdall, the Watcher for the Gods.

Then Freya stood on Bifröst and wept. Frigga, the queenly Goddess, heard the sound of her weeping, and came out of Asgard to comfort her.

"Ah, what comfort can you give me, Frigga?" cried Freya. "What comfort can you give me when Odur will never be found by one who searches for him?"

"Behold how your daughter, the child Hnossa, has grown," said Frigga. Freya looked up and saw a beautiful maiden standing on Bifröst, the Rainbow Bridge. She was young, more youthful than any of the Vanir or the Asyniur, and her face and her form were so lovely that all hearts became melted when they looked upon her.

And Freya was comforted in her loss. She followed Frigga across Bifröst, the Rainbow Bridge, and came once again into the City of the Gods. In her own palace in Asgard Freya dwelt with Hnossa, her child.

Still she wore round her neck Brisingamen, the necklace that lost her Odur. But now she wore it, not for its splendor, but as a sign of the wrong she had done. She weeps, and her tears become golden drops as they fall on the earth. And by poets who know her story she is called The Beautiful Lady in Tears.

HOW FREY WON GERDA, THE GIANT MAIDEN, AND HOW HE LOST HIS MAGIC SWORD

FREY, chief of the Vanir, longed to have sight of his sister who had been from Asgard for so long. (You must know that this happened during the time when Freya was wandering through the world, seeking her husband, the lost Odur.) Now there was in Asgard a place from which one could overlook the world and have a glimpse of all who wandered there. That place was Hlidskjalf, Odin's lofty Watch-Tower.

High up into the blue of the air that Tower went. Frey came to it and he knew that Odin All-Father was not upon

Hlidskjalf. Only the two wolves, Geri and Freki, that crouched beside Odin's seat at the banquet, were there, and they stood in the way of Frey's entrance to the Tower. But Frey spoke to Geri and Freki in the language of the Gods, and Odin's wolves had to let him pass.

But, as he went up the steps within the Tower, Frey, chief of the Vanir, knew that he was doing a fateful thing. For none of the High Gods, not even Thor, the Defender of Asgard, nor Baldur, the Best-Beloved of the Gods, had ever climbed to the top of that Tower and seated themselves upon the All-Father's seat. "But if I could see my sister once I should be contented," said Frey to himself, "and no harm can come to me if I look out on the world."

He came to the top of Hlidskjalf. He seated himself on Odin's lofty seat. He looked out on the world. He saw Midgard, the World of Men, with its houses and towns, its farms and people. Beyond Midgard he saw Jötunheim, the Realm of the Giants, terrible with its dark mountains and its masses of snow and ice. He saw Freya as she went upon her wanderings, and he marked that her face was turned toward Asgard and that her steps were leading toward the City of the Gods. "I have contented myself by looking from Hlidskjalf," said Frey to himself, "and no harm has come to me."

But even as he spoke his gaze was drawn to a dwelling that stood in the middle of the ice and snow of Jötunheim. Long he gazed upon that dwelling without knowing why he looked that way. Then the door of the house was opened and a Giant maiden stood within the doorway. Frey gazed and gazed on her. So great was the beauty of her face that it was like starlight in that dark land. She looked from the doorway of the house, and then turned and went within, shutting the door.

Frey sat on Odin's high seat for long. Then he went down the steps of the Tower and passed by the two wolves, Geri and Freki, that looked threateningly upon him. He went through Asgard, but he found no one to please him in the City of the Gods. That night sleep did not come to him, for his thoughts were fixed upon the loveliness of the Giant maid he had looked upon. And when morning came he was filled with loneliness because he thought himself so far from her. He went to Hlidskjalf again, thinking to climb the Tower and have sight of her once more. But now the two wolves, Geri and Freki, bared their teeth at him and would not let him pass, although he spoke to them again in the language of the Gods.

He went and spoke to wise Niörd, his father. "She whom you have seen, my son," said Niörd, "is Gerda, the daughter of the Giant Gymer. You must give over thinking of her. Your love for her would be an ill thing for you."

"Why should it be an ill thing for me?" Frey asked.

"Because you would have to give that which you prize most for the sake of coming to her."

"That which I prize most," said Frey, "is my magic sword."

"You will have to give your magic sword," said his father, the wise Niörd.

"I will give it," said Frey, loosening his magic sword from his belt.

"Bethink thee, my son," said Niörd. "If thou givest

thy sword, what weapon wilt thou have on the day of Ragnarök, when the Giants will make war upon the Gods?"

Frey did not speak, but he thought the day of Ragnarök was far off. "I cannot live without Gerda," he said, as he turned away.

There was one in Asgard who was called Skirnir. He was a venturesome being who never cared what he said or did. To no one else but Skirnir could Frey bring himself to tell of the trouble that had fallen on him — the trouble that was the punishment for his placing himself on the seat of the All-Father.

Skirnir laughed when he heard Frey's tale. "Thou, a Van, in love with a maid of Jötunheim! This is fun indeed! Will ye make a marriage of it?"

"Would that I might even speak to her or send a message of love to her," said Frey. "But I may not leave my watch over the Elves."

"And if I should take a message to Gerda," said Skirnir the Venturesome, "what would my reward be?"

"My boat Skidbladnir or my boar Golden Bristle," said Frey.

"No, no," said Skirnir. "I want something to go by my side. I want something to use in my hand. Give me the magic sword you own."

Frey thought upon what his father said, that he would be left weaponless on the day of Ragnarök, when the Giants would make war upon the Gods and when Asgard would be endangered. He thought upon this, and drew back from Skirnir, and for a while he remained in thought. And all the time thick-set Skirnir was laughing at him out of his wide mouth and his blue eyes. Then Frey said to himself, "The day of Ragnarök is far off, and I cannot live without Gerda."

He drew the magic sword from his belt and he placed it in Skirnir's hand. "I give you my sword, Skirnir," he said. "Take my message to Gerda, Gymer's daughter. Show her this gold and these precious jewels, and say I love her, and that I claim her love."

"I shall bring the maid to you," said Skirnir the Venturesome.

"But how wilt thou get to Jötunheim?" said Frey, suddenly remembering how dark the Giants' land was and how terrible were the approaches to it.

"Oh, with a good horse and a good sword one can get anywhere," said Skirnir. "My horse is a mighty horse, and you have given me your sword of magic. Tomorrow I shall make the journey."

Skirnir rode across Bifröst, the Rainbow Bridge, laughing out of his wide mouth and his blue eyes at Heimdall, the Warder of the Bridge to Asgard. His mighty horse trod the earth of Midgard, and swam the river that divides Midgard, the World of Men, from Jötunheim, the Realm of the Giants. He rode on heedlessly and recklessly, as he did all things. Then out of the iron forests came the monstrous wolves of Jötunheim, to tear and devour him and his mighty horse. It was well for Skirnir that he had in his belt Frey's magic sword. Its edge slew and its gleam frighted the monstrous beasts. On and on Skirnir rode on his mighty horse. Then he came to a wall of fire. No other horse but his mighty horse could go through it. Skirnir rode through the fire and came to the dale in which was Gymer's dwelling.

And now he was before the house that Frey had seen Gerda enter on the day when he had climbed Hlidskjalf, Odin's Watch-Tower. The mighty hounds that guarded Gymer's dwelling came and bayed around him. But the gleam of the magic sword kept them away. Skirnir backed his horse to the door, and made his horse's hooves strike against it.

Gymer was in the feast hall drinking with his Giant friends, and he did not hear the baying of the hounds nor the clatter that Skirnir made before the door. But Gerda sat spinning with her maidens in the hall. "Who comes to Gymer's door?" she said.

"A warrior upon a mighty horse," said one of the maidens.

"Even though he be an enemy and one who slew my brother, yet shall we open the door to him and give him a cup of Gymer's mead," said Gerda.

One of the maidens opened the door and Skirnir entered Gymer's dwelling. He knew Gerda amongst her maidens. He went to her and showed her the rich gold and the precious jewels that he had brought from Frey. "These are for you, fairest Gerda," he said, "if you will give your love to Frey, the Chief of the Vanir."

"Show your gold and jewels to other maidens," said Gerda. "Gold and jewels will never bring me to give my love."

Then Skirnir the Venturesome, the heedless of his words, drew the magic sword from his belt and held it above her. "Give your love to Frey, who has given me this sword," he said, "or meet your death by the edge of it."

Gerda, Gymer's daughter, only laughed at the reckless Skirnir. "Make the daughters of men fearful by the sharpness of Frey's sword," she said, "but do not try to frighten a Giant's daughter with it."

Then Skirnir the Reckless, the heedless of his words, made the magic sword flash before her eyes, while he cried out in a terrible voice, saying a spell over her:

> Gerda, I will curse thee;
> Yes, with this magic
> Blade I shall touch thee;
> Such is its power
> That, like a thistle,
> Withered 'twill leave thee,
> Like a thistle the wind
> Strips from the roof.

Hearing these terrible words and the strange hissings of the magic sword, Gerda threw herself on the ground, crying out for pity. But Skirnir stood above her, and the magic sword flashed and hissed over her. Skirnir sang:

More ugly I'll leave thee
Than maid ever was;
Thou wilt be mocked at
By men and by Giants;
A Dwarf only will wed thee;
Now on this instant
With this blade I shall touch thee,
And leave thee bespelled.

She lifted herself on her knees and cried out to Skirnir to spare her from the spell of the magic sword.

"Only if thou wilt give thy love to Frey," said Skirnir.

"I will give my love to him," said Gerda. "Now put up thy magic sword and drink a cup of mead and depart from Gymer's dwelling."

"I will not drink a cup of your mead nor shall I depart from Gymer's dwelling until you yourself say that you will meet and speak with Frey."

"I will meet and speak with him," said Gerda.

"When will you meet and speak with him?" asked Skirnir.

"In the wood of Barri nine nights from this. Let him come and meet me there."

Then Skirnir put up his magic sword and drank the cup of mead that Gerda gave him. He rode from Gymer's house, laughing aloud at having won Gerda for Frey, and so making the magic sword his own for ever.

Skirnir the Venturesome, the heedless of his words, riding across Bifröst on his mighty horse, found Frey standing waiting for him beside Heimdall, the Warder of the Bridge to Asgard.

"What news dost thou bring me?" cried Frey. "Speak, Skirnir, before thou dost dismount from thine horse."

"In nine nights from this thou mayst meet Gerda in Barri Wood," said Skirnir. He looked at him, laughing out of his wide mouth and his blue eyes. But Frey turned away, saying to himself:

> Long is one day;
> Long, long two.
> Can I live through
> Nine long days?

Long indeed were these days for Frey. But the ninth day came, and in the evening Frey went to Barri Wood. And there he met Gerda, the Giant maid. She was as fair as when he had seen her before the door of Gymer's house. And when she saw Frey, so tall and noble looking, the Giant's daughter was glad that Skirnir the Venturesome had made her promise to come to Barri Wood. They gave each other rings of gold. It was settled that the Giant maid should come as a bride to Asgard.

Gerda came, but another Giant maid came also. This is how that came to be:

All the Dwellers in Asgard were standing before the great gate, waiting to welcome the bride of Frey. There appeared a Giant maid who was not Gerda; all in armor was she.

"I am Skadi," she said, "the daughter of Thiassi. My father met his death at the hands of the Dwellers in Asgard. I claim a recompense."

"What recompense would you have, maiden?" asked Odin, smiling to see a Giant maid standing so boldly in Asgard.

"A husband from amongst you, even as Gerda. And I myself must be let choose him."

All laughed aloud at the words of Skadi. Then said Odin, laughing, "We will let you choose a husband from amongst us, but you must choose him by his feet."

"I will choose him whatever way you will," said Skadi, fixing her eyes on Baldur, the most beautiful of all the Dwellers in Asgard.

They put a bandage round her eyes, and the Æsir and the Vanir seat in a half circle around. As she went by she stooped over each and laid hands upon their feet. At last she came to one whose feet were so finely formed that she felt sure it was Baldur. She stood up and said:

"This is the one that Skadi chooses for her husband."

Then the Æsir and the Vanir laughed more and more. They took the bandage off her eyes and she saw, not Baldur the Beautiful, but Niörd, the father of Frey. But as Skadi looked more and more on Niörd she became more and more contented with her choice; for Niörd was strong, and he was noble looking.

These two, Niörd and Skadi, went first to live in Niörd's palace by the sea; but the coming of the sea mew would waken Skadi too early in the morning, and she drew her husband to the mountaintop where she was more at home. He would not live long away from the sound of the sea. Back and forward, between the mountain and the sea, Skadi and Niörd went. But Gerda stayed in Asgard with Frey, her husband, and the Æsir and the Vanir came to love greatly Gerda, the Giant maid.

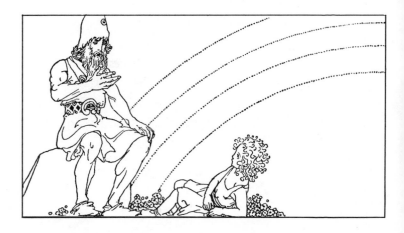

HEIMDALL AND LITTLE HNOSSA:
HOW ALL THINGS CAME TO BE

HNOSSA, the child of Freya and the lost Odur, was the youngest of all the Dwellers in Asgard. And because it had been prophesied that the child would bring her father and her mother together, little Hnossa was often taken without the City of the Gods to stand by Bifröst, the Rainbow Bridge, so that she might greet Odur if his steps turned toward Asgard.

In all the palaces of the City of the Gods little Hnossa was made welcome: in Fensalir, the Halls of Mists, where Frigga, the wife of Odin All-Father, sat spinning with golden threads; in Breidablik, where Baldur, the Well Beloved, lived with his fair wife, the young Nanna; in Bilskirnir, the Winding House, where Thor and Sif lived;

and in Odin's own palace Valaskjalf, that was all roofed over with silver shields.

The greatest of all the palaces was Gladsheim, that was built by the golden-leaved wood, Glasir. Here the banquets of the Gods were held. Often little Hnossa looked within and saw Odin All-Father seated at the banquet table, with a mantle of blue over him and a shining helmet shaped like an eagle upon his head. Odin would sit there, not eating at all, but drinking the wine of the Gods, and taking the food off the table and giving it to Geri and Freki, the two wolves that crouched beside his seat.

She loved to go outside the great gate and stay beside Heimdall, the Warder of the Rainbow Bridge. There, when there was no one crossing that she might watch, she would sit beside Heimdall and listen to the wonders that he spoke of.

Heimdall held in his hands the horn that was called the Gialarhorn. He would sound it to let the Dwellers in Asgard know that one was crossing the Rainbow Bridge. And Heimdall told little Hnossa how he had trained himself to hear the grasses grow, and how he could see all around him for a hundred miles. He could see in the night as well as the day. He never slept. He had nine mothers, he told Hnossa, and he fed on the strength of the earth and the cold sea.

As she sat beside him day after day, Heimdall would tell little Hnossa how all things began. He had lived from the beginning of time and he knew all things. "Before Asgard was built," he said, "and before Odin lived, earth and sea and sky were all mixed together: what was then was the Chasm of Chasms. In the North there was Niflheim, the Place of Deadly Cold. In the South there was Muspelheim, the Land of Fire. In Niflheim there was a cauldron called Hveigilmer that poured out twelve rivers that flowed into the Chasm of Chasms.

"Ginnungagap, the Chasm of Chasms, filled up with ice, for the waters of the rivers froze as they poured into it. From Muspelheim came clouds of fire that turned the ice into thick mists. The mists fell down again in drops of dew, and from these drops were formed Ymir, the Ancient Giant.

"Ymir, the Ancient Giant, traveled along by the twelve rivers until he came to where another living form was standing in the mists. This was a Giant Cow. Audhumla was the name of that cow. Ymir lay down beside her and drank her milk, and on the milk she gave him he lived. Other beings were formed out of the dew that fell to the ground. They were the Daughters of the Frost, and Ymir, the Ancient Giant, married one, and their children were the Giants.

"One day Ymir saw Audhumla breathe upon a cliff of ice and lick with her tongue the place she breathed on. As her tongue went over and over the place he saw that a figure was being formed. It was not like a Giant's form; it was more shapely and more beautiful. A head appeared in the cliff and golden hair fell over the ice. As Ymir looked upon the being that was being formed he hated him for his beauty.

"Audhumla, the Giant Cow, went on licking the place where she had breathed. At last a man completely formed stepped from the cliff. Ymir, the Ancient Giant, hated him so much that he would have slain him then and there. But he knew that if he did this, Audhumla would feed him no more with her milk.

"Bur was the name of the man who was formed in the ice cliff, Bur, the first of the heroes. He, too, lived on the milk of Audhumla. He married a daughter of the Ancient Giant and he had a son. But Ymir and Ymir's sons hated Bur, and the time came at last when they were able to kill him.

"And now there was war between Ymir and Ymir's sons and the son and son's sons of Bur. Odin was the son of Bur's son. Odin brought all his brothers together, and they were able to destroy Ymir and all his brood — all except one. So huge was Ymir that when he was slain his blood poured out in such a mighty flood that his sons were all drowned in it, all except Bergelmir, who was in a boat with his wife when the flood came, and who floated away on the flood to the place that we now call Jötunheim, the Realm of the Giants.

"Now Odin and his sons took the body of Ymir — the vastest body that ever was — and they flung it into the Chasm of Chasms, filling up all the hollow places with it. They dug the bones out of the body and they piled them up as the mountains. They took the teeth out and they made them into the rocks. They took the hair of Ymir and they made it into the forests of trees. They took his eyebrows and formed them into the place where Men now dwell, Midgard. And out of Ymir's hollow skull they made the sky.

"And Odin and his sons and brothers did more than this. They took the sparks and the clouds of flame that blew from Muspelheim, and they made them into the sun and the moon and all the stars that are in the sky. Odin found a dusky Giantess named Night whose son was called Day, and he gave both of them horses to drive across the sky. Night drove a horse that is named Hrimfaxe, Frosty Mane, and Day drove a horse that is named Skinfaxe, Shining Mane. From Hrimfaxe's bit fall the drops that make the dew upon the earth.

"Then Odin and his sons made a race of men and women and gave them Midgard to live in. Ugly Dwarfs had grown up and had spread themselves over the earth. These Odin made go live in the hollow places beneath the earth. The Elves he let stay on the earth, but he gave them the tasks of tending the streams and the grasses and the flowers. And with the Vanir he made peace after a war had been waged, taking Niörd from them for a hostage.

"Bergelmir, the Giant who escaped drowning in Ymir's blood, had sons and daughters in Jötunheim. They hated Odin and his sons and strove against them. When Odin lighted up the world with the sun and the moon they were very wroth, and they found two of the fiercest of the mighty wolves of Jötunheim and set them to follow them. And still the sun and the moon, Sol and Mani, are followed by the wolves of Jötunheim."

Such wonders did Heimdall with the Golden Teeth tell

Hnossa, the youngest of the Dwellers in Asgard. Often the child stayed with him by the Rainbow Bridge, and saw the Gods pass to and from Midgard: Thor, with his crown of stars, with the great hammer Miölnir in his hands, with the gloves of iron that he used when he grasped Miölnir; Thor in his chariot drawn by two goats and wearing the belt that doubled his strength; Frigga, with her dress of falcon feathers, flying swiftly as a bird; Odin All-Father himself, riding upon Sleipner, his eight-legged steed, clad all in golden armor, with his golden helmet, shaped like an eagle, upon his head, and with his spear Gungnir in his hand.

Heimdall kept his horn in the branch of a great tree. This tree was called Ygdrassil, he told little Hnossa, and it was a wonder to Gods and Men. "No one knows of a time when Ygdrassil was not growing, and all are afraid to speak of the time when it will be destroyed.

"Ygdrassil has three roots. One goes deep under Midgard, another goes deep under Jötunheim, and the third grows above Asgard. Over Odin's hall a branch of Ygdrassil grows, and it is called the Peace Bough.

"You see Ygdrassil, little Hnossa, but you do not know all the wonders of it. Far up in its branches four stags graze; they shake from their horns the water that falls as rain upon the earth. On the topmost branch of Ygdrassil, the branch that is so high that the Gods themselves can hardly see it, there is an eagle that knows all things. Upon the beak of this eagle a hawk is perched, a hawk that sees what the eyes of the eagle may not see.

"The root of Ygdrassil that is in Midgard goes deep

down to the place of the dead. Here there is an evil dragon named Nidhögg that gnaws constantly at the root, striving to destroy Ygdrassil, the Tree of trees. And Ratatösk, the Squirrel of Mischief — behold him now! — runs up and down Ygdrassil, making trouble between the eagle above and the dragon below. He goes to tell the dragon how the eagle is bent upon tearing him to pieces and he goes back to tell the eagle how the dragon plans to devour him. The stories that he brings to Nidhögg make that evil dragon more fierce to destroy Ygdrassil, the Tree of trees, so that he may come upon the eagle and devour him.

"There are two wells by the roots of Ygdrassil, and one is above and one is below. One is beside the root that grows in Jötunheim. This is a Well of Knowledge, and it is guarded by old Mimir the Wise. Whoever drinks out of this well knows of all the things that will come to be. The other well is by the root that grows above Asgard. No one may drink out of this well. The three sisters that are the holy Norns guard it, and they take the white water from it to water Ygdrassil, that the Tree of Life may keep green and strong. This well, little Hnossa, is called Urda's Well."

And little Hnossa heard that by Urda's Well there were two beautiful white swans. They made a music that the Dwellers in Asgard often heard. But Hnossa was too young to hear the music that was made by the swans of Urda's Well.

THE ALL-FATHER'S FOREBODINGS:
HOW HE LEAVES ASGARD

TWO ravens had Odin All-Father; Hugin and Munin were their names; they flew through all the worlds every day, and coming back to Asgard they would light on Odin's shoulders and tell him of all the things they had seen and heard. And once a day passed without the ravens coming back. Then Odin, standing on the Watch-Tower Hlidskjalf, said to himself:

> I fear me for Hugin,
> Lest he come not back,
> But I watch more for Munin.

A day passed and the ravens flew back. They sat, one on each of his shoulders. Then did the All-Father go into the

Council Hall that was beside Glasir, the wood that had leaves of gold, and harken to what Hugin and Munin had to tell him.

They told him only of shadows and forebodings. Odin All-Father did not speak to the Dwellers in Asgard of the things they told him. But Frigga, his Queen, saw in his eyes the shadows and forebodings of things to come. And when he spoke to her about these things she said, "Do not strive against what must take place. Let us go to the holy Norns who sit by Urda's Well and see if the shadows and the forebodings will remain when you have looked into their eyes."

And so it came that Odin and the Gods left Asgard and came to Urda's Well, where, under the great root of Ygdrassil, the three Norns sat, with the two fair swans below them. Odin went, and Tyr, the great swordsman, and Baldur, the most beautiful and the Best-Beloved of the Gods, and Thor, with his Hammer.

A Rainbow Bridge went from Asgard, the City of the Gods, to Midgard, the World of Men. But another Rainbow Bridge, more beautiful and more tremulous still, went from Asgard to that root of Ygdrassil under which was Urda's Well. This Rainbow Bridge was seldom seen by men. And where the ends of the two rainbows came together Heimdall stood, Heimdall with the Golden Teeth, the Watcher for the Gods, and the Keeper of the Way to Urda's Well.

"Open the gate, Heimdall," said the All-Father, "open the gate, for today the Gods would visit the holy Norns."

Without a word Heimdall opened wide the gate that

led to that bridge more colored and more tremulous than any rainbow seen from earth. Then did Odin and Tyr and Baldur step out on the bridge. Thor followed, but before his foot was placed on the bridge, Heimdall laid his hand upon him.

"The others may go, but you may not go that way, Thor," said Heimdall.

"What? Would you, Heimdall, hold me back?" said Thor.

"Yes, for I am Keeper of the Way to the Norns," said Heimdall. "You with the mighty hammer you carry are too weighty for this way. The bridge I guard would break under you, Thor with the hammer."

"Nevertheless I will go visit the Norns with Odin and my comrades," said Thor.

"But not this way, Thor," said Heimdall. "I will not let the bridge be broken under the weight of you and your hammer. Leave your hammer here with me if you would go this way."

"No, no," said Thor. "I will not leave in any one's charge the hammer that defends Asgard. And I may not be turned back from going with Odin and my comrades."

"There is another way to Urda's Well," said Heimdall. "Behold these two great Cloud Rivers, Körmt and Ermt. Canst thou wade through them? They are cold and suffocating, but they will bring thee to Urda's Well, where sit the three holy Norns."

Thor looked out on the two great rolling rivers of cloud. It was a bad way for one to go, cold and suffocating. Yet if he went that way he could keep on his shoulder the hammer which he would not leave in another's charge. He stept out into the Cloud River that flowed by the Rainbow Bridge, and with his hammer upon his shoulder he went struggling on to the other river.

Odin, Tyr, and Baldur were beside Urda's Well when Thor came struggling out of the Cloud River, wet and choking, but with his hammer still upon his shoulder. There stood Tyr, upright and handsome, leaning on his sword that was inscribed all over with magic runes; there stood Baldur, smiling, with his head bent as he listened to the murmur of the two fair swans; and there stood Odin All-Father, clad in his blue cloak fringed with golden stars, without the eagle-helmet upon his head, and with no spear in his hands.

The three Norns, Urda, Verdandi, and Skulda, sat beside the well that was in the hollow of the great root of Ygdrassil. Urda was ancient and with white hair, and Verdandi was beautiful, while Skulda could hardly be seen, for she sat far back, and her hair fell over her face and eyes. Urda, Verdandi, and Skulda; they knew the whole of the Past, the whole of the Present, and the whole of the Future. Odin, looking on them, saw into the eyes of Skulda even. Long, long he stood looking on the Norns with the eyes of a God, while the others listened to the murmur of the swans and the falling of the leaves of Ygdrassil into Urda's Well.

Looking into their eyes, Odin saw the shadows and forebodings that Hugin and Munin told him of take shape and substance. And now others came across the Rainbow Bridge. They were Frigga and Sif and Nanna, the wives of Odin and Thor and Baldur. Frigga looked upon the Norns. As she did, she turned a glance of love and sadness upon Baldur, her son, and then she drew back and placed her hand upon Nanna's head.

Odin turned from gazing on the Norns, and looked upon Frigga, his queenly wife. "I would leave Asgard for a while, wife of Odin," he said.

"Yea," said Frigga. "Much has to be done in Midgard, the World of Men."

"I would change what knowledge I have into wisdom," said Odin, "so that the things that are to happen will be changed into the best that may be."

"You would go to Mimir's Well," said Frigga.

"I would go to Mimir's Well," said Odin.

"My husband, go," said Frigga.

Then they went back over that Rainbow Bridge that is more beautiful and more tremulous than the one that men see from the earth; they went back over the Rainbow Bridge, the Æsir and the Asyniur, Odin and Frigga, Baldur and Nanna, Tyr, with his sword, and Sif beside Tyr. As for Thor, he went struggling through the Cloud Rivers Körmt and Ermt, his hammer Miölnir upon his shoulder.

Little Hnossa, the youngest of the Dwellers in Asgard, was there, standing beside Heimdall, the Watcher for the Gods and the Keeper of the Bridge to Urda's Well, when Odin All-Father and Frigga, his Queen, went through the great gate with heads bent. "Tomorrow," Hnossa heard Odin say, "tomorrow I shall be Vegtam the Wanderer upon the ways of Midgard and Jötunheim."

PART II

ODIN THE WANDERER

ODIN GOES TO MIMIR'S WELL:
HIS SACRIFICE FOR WISDOM

A ND so Odin, no longer riding on Sleipner, his eight-
legged steed; no longer wearing his golden armor
and his eagle-helmet, and without even his spear in his
hand, traveled through Midgard, the World of Men, and
made his way toward Jötunheim, the Realm of the Giants.

No longer was he called Odin All-Father, but Vegtam
the Wanderer. He wore a cloak of dark blue and he carried a traveler's staff in his hands. And now, as he went
toward Mimir's Well, which was near to Jötunheim, he
came upon a Giant riding on a great Stag.

Odin seemed a man to men and a giant to giants. He

went beside the Giant on the great Stag and the two talked together. "Who art thou, O brother?" Odin asked the Giant.

"I am Vafthrudner, the wisest of the Giants," said the one who was riding on the Stag. Odin knew him then. Vafthrudner was indeed the wisest of the Giants, and many went to strive to gain wisdom from him. But those who went to him had to answer the riddles Vafthrudner asked, and if they failed to answer the Giant took their heads off.

"I am Vegtam the Wanderer," Odin said, "and I know who thou art, O Vafthrudner. I would strive to learn something from thee."

The Giant laughed, showing his teeth. "Ho, ho," he said, "I am ready for a game with thee. Dost thou know the stakes? My head to thee if I cannot answer any question thou wilt ask. And if thou canst not answer any question that I may ask, then thy head goes to me. Ho, ho, ho. And now let us begin."

"I am ready," Odin said.

"Then tell me," said Vafthrudner, "tell me the name of the river that divides Asgard from Jötunheim?"

"Ifling is the name of that river," said Odin. "Ifling that is dead cold, yet never frozen."

"Thou hast answered rightly, O Wanderer," said the Giant. "But thou hast still to answer other questions. What are the names of the horses that Day and Night drive across the sky?"

"Skinfaxe and Hrimfaxe," Odin answered. Vafthrudner

was startled to hear one say the names that were known only to the Gods and to the wisest of the Giants. There was only one question now that he might ask before it came to the stranger's turn to ask him questions.

"Tell me," said Vafthrudner, "what is the name of the plain on which the last battle will be fought?"

"The Plain of Vigard," said Odin, "the plain that is a hundred miles long and a hundred miles across."

It was now Odin's turn to ask Vafthrudner questions. "What will be the last words that Odin will whisper into the ear of Baldur, his dear son?" he asked.

Very startled was the Giant Vafthrudner at that question. He sprang to the ground and looked at the stranger keenly.

"Only Odin knows what his last words to Baldur will be," he said, "and only Odin would have asked that question. Thou art Odin, O Wanderer, and thy question I cannot answer."

"Then," said Odin, "if thou wouldst keep thy head, answer me this: what price will Mimir ask for a draught from the Well of Wisdom that he guards?"

"He will ask thy right eye as a price, O Odin," said Vafthrudner.

"Will he ask no less a price than that?" said Odin.

"He will ask no less a price. Many have come to him for a draught from the Well of Wisdom, but no one yet has given the price Mimir asks. I have answered thy question, O Odin. Now give up thy claim to my head and let me go on my way."

"I give up my claim to thy head," said Odin. Then Vafthrudner, the wisest of the Giants, went on his way, riding on his great Stag.

It was a terrible price that Mimir would ask for a draught from the Well of Wisdom, and very troubled was Odin All-Father when it was revealed to him. His right eye! For all time to be without the sight of his right eye! Almost he would have turned back to Asgard, giving up his quest for wisdom.

He went on, turning neither to Asgard nor to Mimir's Well. And when he went toward the South he saw Muspelheim, where stood Surtur with the Flaming Sword, a terrible figure, who would one day join the Giants in their war against the Gods. And when he turned North he heard the roaring of the cauldron Hvergelmer as it poured itself out of Niflheim, the place of darkness and dread. And Odin knew that the world must not be left between Surtur, who would destroy it with fire, and Niflheim, that would gather it back to Darkness and Nothingness. He, the eldest of the Gods, would have to win the wisdom that would help to save the world.

And so, with his face stern in front of his loss and pain, Odin All-Father turned and went toward Mimir's Well. It was under the great root of Ygdrassil — the root that grew out of Jötunheim. And there sat Mimir, the Guardian of the Well of Wisdom, with his deep eyes bent upon the deep water. And Mimir, who had drunk every day from the Well of Wisdom, knew who it was that stood before him.

"Hail, Odin, Eldest of the Gods," he said.

Then Odin made reverence to Mimir, the wisest of the world's beings. "I would drink from your well, Mimir," he said.

"There is a price to be paid. All who have come here to drink have shrunk from paying that price. Will you, Eldest of the Gods, pay it?"

"I will not shrink from the price that has to be paid, Mimir," said Odin All-Father.

"Then drink," said Mimir. He filled up a great horn with water from the well and gave it to Odin.

Odin took the horn in both his hands and drank and drank. And as he drank all the future became clear to him. He saw all the sorrows and troubles that would fall upon Men and Gods. But he saw, too, why the sorrows and troubles had to fall, and he saw how they might be borne so that Gods and Men, by being noble in the days of sorrow and trouble, would leave in the world a force that one day, a day that was far off indeed, would destroy the evil that brought terror and sorrow and despair into the world.

Then when he had drunk out of the great horn that Mimir had given him, he put his hand to his face and he plucked out his right eye. Terrible was the pain that Odin All-Father endured. But he made no groan nor moan. He bowed his head and put his cloak before his face, as Mimir took the eye and let it sink deep, deep into the water of the Well of Wisdom. And there the Eye of Odin stayed, shining up through the water, a sign to all who came to that place of the price that the Father of the Gods had paid for his wisdom.

ODIN FACES AN EVIL MAN

ONCE, when his wisdom was less great, Odin had lived in the world of men. Frigga, his Queen, was with him then; they had lived on a bleak island, and they were known as Grimner the Fisherman and his wife.

Always Odin and Frigga were watching over the sons of men, watching to know which ones they would foster and train so that they might have the strength and spirit to save the world from the power of the Giants. And while they were staying on the bleak island, Odin and Frigga saw the sons of King Hrauding, and both thought that in them the spirit of heroes could be fostered. Odin and Frigga made plans to bring the children to them, so that they might be under their care and training. One day the boys went fishing. A storm came and drove their boat on the rocks of the island where Odin and Frigga lived.

They brought them to their hut, Odin and Frigga, and they told them they would care for them and train them through the winter and that in the spring they would build a boat that would carry them back to their father's country. "We shall see," said Odin to Frigga that night, "we shall see which of the two can be formed into the noblest hero."

He said that because Frigga favored one of the boys and he favored the other. Frigga thought well of the elder boy, Agnar, who had a gentle voice and quiet and kindly ways. But Odin thought more of the younger boy. Geirrod, his name was, and he was strong and passionate, with a high and a loud voice.

Odin took Geirrod into his charge, and he showed him how to fish and hunt. He made the boy even bolder than he was by making him leap from rock to rock, and by letting him climb the highest cliffs and jump across the widest chasms. He would bring him to the den of the bear and make him fight for his life with the spear he had made for him. Agnar went to the chase, too, and showed his skill and boldness. But Geirrod overcame him in nearly every trial. "What a hero Geirrod will be," Odin would often say.

Agnar stayed often with Frigga. He would stay beside her while she spun, listening to the tales she told, and asking such questions as brought him more and more wisdom. And Agnar heard of Asgard and of the Dwellers in

Asgard and of how they protected Midgard, the World of Men, from the Giants of Jötunheim. Agnar, though he did not speak out, said in his own mind that he would give all his life and all his strength and all his thought to helping the work of the Gods.

Spring came and Odin built a boat for Geirrod and Agnar. They could go back now to their own country. And before they set out Odin told Geirrod that one day he would come to visit him. "And do not be too proud to receive a Fisherman in your hall, Geirrod," said Odin. "A King should give welcome to the poorest who comes to his hall."

"I will be a hero, no doubt of that," Geirrod answered. "And I would be a King, too, only Agnar Little-good was born before me."

Agnar bade goodby to Frigga and to Odin, thanking them for the care they had taken of Geirrod and himself. He looked into Frigga's eyes, and he told her that he would strive to learn how he might fight the battle for the Gods.

The two went into the boat and they rowed away. They came near to King Hrauding's realm. They saw the castle overlooking the sea. Then Geirrod did a terrible thing. He turned the boat back toward the sea, and he cast the oars away. Then, for he was well fit to swim the roughest sea and climb the highest cliffs, he plunged into the water and struck out toward the shore. And Agnar, left without oars, went drifting out to sea.

Geirrod climbed the high cliffs and came to his father's castle.

King Hrauding, who had given up both of his sons for lost, was rejoiced to see him. Geirrod told of Agnar that he had fallen out of the boat on their way back and that he had been drowned. King Hrauding, who had thought both of his sons were gone from him, was glad enough that one had come safe. He put Geirrod beside him on the throne, and when he died Geirrod was made King over the people.

And now Odin, having drunk from Mimir's Well, went through the kingdoms of men, judging Kings and simple people according to the wisdom he had gained. He came at last to the kingdom that Geirrod ruled over. Odin thought that of all the Kings he had judged to be noble, Geirrod would assuredly be the noblest.

He went to the King's house as a Wanderer, blind of one eye, wearing a cloak of dark blue and with a wanderer's staff in his hands. As he drew near the King's house men on dark horses came riding behind him. The first of the men did not turn his horse as he came near the Wanderer, but rode on, nearly trampling him to the ground.

As they came before the King's house the men on the dark horses shouted for servants. Only one servant was in the stable. He came out and took the horse of the first man. Then the others called upon the Wanderer to tend their horses. He had to hold the stirrups for some of them to dismount.

Odin knew who the first man was. He was Geirrod the King. And he knew who the man who served in the stable was. He was Agnar, Geirrod's brother. By the wisdom he ha gained he knew that Agnar had come back to his father's kingdom in the guise of a servant, and he knew that Geirrod did not know who this servant was.

They went into the stable together. Agnar took bread and broke it and gave some to the Wanderer. He gave him, too, straw to seat himself on. But in a while Odin said, "I would seat myself at the fire in the King's hall and eat my supper of meat."

"Nay, stay here," Agnar said. "I will give you more bread and a wrap to cover yourself with. Do not go to the door of the King's house, for the King is angry today and he might repulse you."

"How?" said Odin. "A King turn away a Wanderer who comes to his door! It cannot be that he would do it!"

"Today he is angry," Agnar said. Again he begged him not to go to the door of the King's house. But Odin rose up from the straw on which he was seated and went to the door.

A porter, hunchbacked and with long arms, stood at the door. "I am a Wanderer, and I would have rest and food in the King's hall," Odin said.

"Not in this King's hall," said the hunchbacked porter. He would have barred the door to Odin, but the voice of the King called him away. Odin then strode into the hall and saw the King at table with his friends, all dark-bearded, and cruel-looking men. And when Odin looked on them he knew that the boy whom he had trained in nobility had become a King over robbers.

"Since you have come into the hall where we eat, sing to us, Wanderer," shouted one of the dark men. "Aye, I will sing to you," said Odin. Then he stood between two of the stone pillars in the hall and he sang a song reproaching the King for having fallen into an evil way of life, and denouncing all for following the cruel ways of robbers.

"Seize him," said the King, when Odin's song was finished. The dark men threw themselves upon Odin and put chains around him and bound him between the stone pillars of the hall. "He came into this hall for warmth, and warmth he shall have," said Geirrod. He called upon his servants to heap up wood around him. They did this. Then the King, with his own hand, put a blazing torch to the wood and the fagots blazed up around the Wanderer.

The fagots burned round and round him. But the fire did not burn the flesh of Odin All-Father. The King and the King's friends stood round, watching with delight the fires blaze round a living man. The fagots all burned away, and Odin was left standing there with his terrible gaze fixed upon the men who were so hard and cruel.

They went to sleep, leaving him chained to the pillars of the hall. Odin could have broken the chains and pulled down the pillars, but he wanted to see what else would happen in this King's house. The servants were ordered not to bring food or drink to him, but at dawn, when there was no one near, Agnar came to him with a horn of ale and gave it to him to drink.

The next evening when the King came back from his robberies, and when he and his friends, sitting down at the tables, had eaten like wolves, he ordered the fagots to be placed around Odin. And again they stood around, watching in delight the fire playing around a living man. And as before Odin stood there, unhurt by the fire, and his steady and terrible gaze made the King hate him more and more. And all day he was kept in chains, and the servants were forbidden to bring him food or drink. None knew that a horn of ale was brought to him at dawn.

And night after night, for eight nights, this went on. Then, on the ninth night, when the fires around him had been lighted, Odin lifted up his voice and began to sing a song.

His song became louder and louder, and the King and the King's friends and the servants of the King's house had to stand still and harken to it. Odin sang about Geirrod, the King; how the Gods had protected him, giving him strength and skill, and how instead of making a noble use of that strength and skill he had made himself like one of the wild beasts. Then he sang of how the vengeance of the Gods was about to fall on this ignoble King.

The flames died down and Geirrod and his friends saw before them, not a friendless Wanderer, but one who looked more kingly than any King of the earth. The chains fell down from his body and he advanced toward the evil company. Then Geirrod rushed upon him with his sword in hand to kill him. The sword struck him, but Odin remained unhurt.

> Thy life runs out,
> The Gods they are wroth with thee;
> Draw near if thou canst;
> Odin thou shalt see.

So Odin sang, and, in fear of his terrible gaze, Geirrod and his company shrank away. And as they shrank away they were changed into beasts, into the wolves that range the forests.

And Agnar came forward, and him Odin declared to be King. All the folk were glad when Agnar came to rule over them, for they had been oppressed by Geirrod in his cruel reign. And Agnar was not only kind, but he was strong and victorious in his rule.

ODIN WINS FOR MEN THE MAGIC MEAD

IT was the Dwarfs who brewed the Magic Mead, and it was the Giants who hid it away. But it was Odin who brought it from the place where it was hidden and gave it to the sons of men. Those who drank of the Magic Mead became very wise, and not only that but they could put their wisdom into such beautiful words that every one who heard would love and remember it.

The Dwarfs brewed the Magic Mead through cruelty and villainy. They made it out of the blood of a man. The man was Kvasir the Poet. He had wisdom, and he had such beautiful words with it, that what he said was loved and remembered by all. The Dwarfs brought Kvasir down into their caverns and they killed him there. "Now," they said, "we have Kvasir's blood and Kvasir's wisdom. No one else will have his wisdom but us." They poured the blood into three jars and they mixed it with honey, and from it they brewed the Magic Mead.

Having killed a man the Dwarfs became more and more bold. They came out of their caverns and went up and down through Midgard, the World of Men. They went into Jötunheim, and began to play their evil tricks on the most harmless of the Giants.

They came upon one Giant who was very simple. Gilling was his name. They persuaded Gilling to row them out to sea in a boat. Then the two most cunning of the Dwarfs, Galar and Fialar, steered the boat on to a rock. The boat split. Gilling, who could not swim, was drowned. The Dwarfs clambered up on pieces of the boat and came safely ashore. They were so delighted with their evil tricks that they wanted to play some more of them.

Galar and Fialar then thought of a new piece of mischief they might do. They led their band of Dwarfs to Gilling's house and screamed out to his wife that Gilling was dead. The Giant's wife began to weep and lament. At last she rushed out of the house weeping and clapping her hands. Now Galar and Fialar had clambered up on the lintel of the house, and as she came running out they cast a millstone on her head. It struck her and Gilling's wife fell down dead. More and more the Dwarfs were delighted at the destruction they were making.

They were so insolent now that they made up songs and sang them, songs that were all a boast of how they had killed Kvasir the Poet, and Gilling the Giant, and Gilling's wife. They stayed around Jötunheim, tormenting all whom they were able to torment, and flattering themselves that they were great and strong. They stayed too long, however. Suttung, Gilling's brother, tracked them down and captured them.

Suttung was not harmless and simple like Gilling, his brother. He was cunning and he was covetous. Once they were in his hands the Dwarfs had no chance of making an escape. He took them and left them on a rock in the sea, a rock that the tide would cover.

The Giant stood up in the water taller than the rock, and the tide as it came in did not rise above his knees. He stood there watching the Dwarfs as the water rose up round them and they became more and more terrified.

"Oh, take us off the rock, good Suttung," they cried out to him. "Take us off the rock and we will give you gold and jewels. Take us off the rock and we will give you a necklace as beautiful as Brisingamen." So they cried out to him, but the Giant Suttung only laughed at them. He had no need of gold or jewels.

Then Fialar and Galar cried out: "Take us off the rock and we will give you the jars of the Magic Mead we have brewed."

"The Magic Mead," said Suttung. "This is something that no one else has. It would be well to get it, for it might help us in the battle against the Gods. Yes, I will get the Magic Mead from them."

He took the band of Dwarfs off the rock, but he held

Galar and Fialar, their chiefs, while the others went into their caverns and brought up the jars of the Magic Mead. Suttung took the Mead and brought it to a cavern in a mountain near his dwelling. And thus it happened that the Magic Mead, brewed by the Dwarfs through cruelty and villainy, came into the hands of the Giants. And the story now tells how Odin, the Eldest of the Gods, at that time in the world as Vegtam the Wanderer, took the Magic Mead out of Suttung's possession and brought it into the world of men.

Now, Suttung had a daughter named Gunnlöd, and she by her goodness and her beauty was like Gerda and Skadi, the Giant maids whom the Dwellers in Asgard favored. Suttung, that he might have a guardian for the Magic Mead, enchanted Gunnlöd, turning her from a beautiful Giant maiden into a witch with long teeth and sharp nails. He shut her into the cavern where the jars of the Magic Mead were hidden.

Odin heard of the death of Kvasir whom he honored above all men. The Dwarfs who slew him he had closed up in their caverns so that they were never again able to come out into the World of Men. And then he set out to get the Magic Mead that he might give it to men, so that, tasting it, they would have wisdom, and words would be at their command that would make wisdom loved and remembered.

How Odin won the Magic Mead out of the rock-covered cavern where Suttung had hidden it, and how he broke the enchantment that lay upon Gunnlöd, Suttung's daughter, is a story often told around the hearths of men.

Nine strong thralls were mowing in a field as a Wanderer went by clad in a dark blue cloak and carrying a wanderer's staff in his hand. One of the thralls spoke to the Wanderer: "Tell them in the house of Baugi up yonder that I can mow no more until a whetstone to sharpen my scythe is sent to me." "Here is a whetstone," said the Wanderer, and he took one from his belt. The thrall who had spoken whetted his scythe with it and began to mow. The grass went down before his scythe as if the wind had cut it. "Give us the whetstone, give us the whetstone," cried the other thralls. The Wanderer threw the whetstone amongst them, leaving them quarreling over it, and went on his way.

The Wanderer came to the house of Baugi, the brother of Suttung. He rested in Baugi's house, and at supper time he was given food at the great table. And while he was eating with the Giant a Messenger from the field came in.

"Baugi," said the Messenger, "your nine thralls are all dead. They killed each other with their scythes, fighting in the field about a whetstone. There are no thralls now to do your work."

"What shall I do, what shall I do?" said Baugi the Giant. "My fields will not be mown now, and I shall have no hay to feed my cattle and my horses in the winter."

"I might work for you," said the Wanderer.

"One man's work is no use to me," said the Giant, "I must have the work of nine men."

"I shall do the work of nine men," said the Wanderer, "give me a trial, and see."

The next day Vegtam the Wanderer went into Baugi's field. He did as much work as the nine thralls had done in a day.

"Stay with me for the season," said Baugi, "and I shall give you a full reward."

So Vegtam stayed at the Giant's house and worked in the Giant's fields, and when all the work of the season was done Baugi said to him:

"Speak now and tell me what reward I am to give you."

"The only reward I shall ask of you," said Vegtam, "is a draught of the Magic Mead."

"The Magic Mead?" said Baugi. "I do not know where it is nor how to get it."

"Your brother Suttung has it. Go to him and claim a draught of the Magic Mead for me."

Baugi went to Suttung. But when he heard what he had come for, the Giant Suttung turned on his brother in a rage.

"A draught of the Magic Mead?" he said. "To no one will I give a draught of the Magic Mead. Have I not enchanted my daughter Gunnlöd, so that she may watch over it? And you tell me that a Wanderer who has done the work of nine men for you asks a draught of the Magic Mead for his fee! O Giant as foolish as Gilling! O oaf of a Giant! Who could have done such work for you, and who would demand such a fee from you, but one of our enemies, the Æsir? Go from me now and never come to me again with talk of the Magic Mead."

Baugi went back to his house and told the Wanderer that Suttung would yield none of the Magic Mead. "I hold you to your bargain," said Vegtam the Wanderer, "and you will have to get me the fee I asked. Come with me now and help me to get it."

He made Baugi bring him to the place where the Magic Mead was hidden. The place was a cavern in the mountain. In front of that cavern was a great mass of stone.

"We cannot move that stone nor get through it," said Baugi. "I cannot help you to your fee."

The Wanderer drew an auger from his belt. "This will bore through the rock if there is strength behind it. You have the strength, Giant. Begin now and bore."

Baugi took the auger in his hands and bored with all his strength, and the Wanderer stood by leaning on his staff, calm and majestic in his cloak of blue.

"I have made a deep, deep hole. It goes through the rock," Baugi said, at last.

The Wanderer went to the hole and blew into it. The dust of the rock flew back into their faces.

"So that is your boasted strength, Giant," he said. "You have not bored half-way through the rock. Work again."

Then Baugi took the auger again and he bored deeper and deeper into the rock. And he blew into it, and lo! His breath went through. Then he looked at the Wanderer to see what he would do; his eyes had become fierce and he held the auger in his hand as if it were a stabbing knife.

"Look up to the head of the rock," said the Wanderer. As Baugi looked up the Wanderer changed himself into a snake and glided into the hole in the rock. And Baugi struck at him with the auger, hoping to kill him, but the snake slipped through.

Behind the mighty rock there was a hollow place all lighted up by the shining crystals in the rock. And within the hollow place there was an ill-looking witch, with long teeth and sharp nails. But she sat there rocking herself and letting tears fall from her eyes. "O youth and beauty," she sang, "O sight of men and women, sad, sad for me it is that you are shut away, and that I have only this closed-in cavern and this horrible form."

A snake glided across the floor. "Oh, that you were deadly and that you might slay me," cried the witch. The snake glided past her. Then she heard a voice speak softly: "Gunnlöd, Gunnlöd!" She looked round, and there standing behind her was a majestic man, clad in a cloak of dark blue, Odin, the Eldest of the Gods.

"You have come to take the Magic Mead that my father has set me here to guard," she cried. "You shall not have it. Rather shall I spill it out on the thirsty earth of the cavern."

"Gunnlöd," he said, and he came to her. She looked at him and she felt the red blood of youth come back into her cheeks. She put her hands with their sharp nails over her breast, and she felt the nails drive into her flesh. "Save me from all this ugliness," she cried.

"I will save you," Odin said. He went to her. He took

her hands and held them. He kissed her on the mouth. All the marks of ill favor went from her. She was no longer bent, but tall and shapely. Her eyes became wide and deep blue. Her mouth became red and her hands soft and beautiful. She became as fair as Gerda, the Giant maid whom Frey had wed.

They stayed looking at each other, then they sat down side by side and talked softly to each other, Odin, the Eldest of the Gods, and Gunnlöd, the beautiful Giant maiden.

She gave him the three jars of the Magic Mead and she told him she would go out of the cavern with him. Three days passed and still they were together. Then Odin by his wisdom found hidden paths and passages that led out of the cavern and he brought Gunnlöd out into the light of the day.

And he brought with him the jars of the Magic Mead, the Mead whose taste gives wisdom, and wisdom in such beautiful words that all love and remember it. And Gunnlöd, who had tasted a little of the Magic Mead, wandered through the world singing of the beauty and the might of Odin, and of her love for him.

ODIN TELLS TO VIDAR, HIS SILENT SON, THE SECRET OF HIS DOINGS

IT was not only to Giants and Men that Odin showed himself in the days when he went through Jötunheim and Midgard as Vegtam the Wanderer. He met and he spoke with the Gods also, with one who lived far away from Asgard and with others who came to Midgard and to Jötunheim.

The one who lived far away from Asgard was Vidar, Odin's silent son. Far within a wilderness, with branches and tall grass growing around him, Vidar sat. And near by him a horse grazed with a saddle upon it, a horse that was ever ready for the speedy journey.

And Odin, now Vegtam the Wanderer, came into that silent place and spoke to Vidar, the Silent God.

"O Vidar," he said, "strangest of all my sons; God who

will live when all of us have passed away; God who will bring the memory of the Dwellers of Asgard into a world that will know not their power; O Vidar, well do I know why there grazes near by thee the horse ever ready for the speedy journey: it is that thou mayst spring upon it and ride unchecked, a son speeding to avenge his father.

"To you only, O Vidar the Silent One, will I speak of the secrets of my doings. Who but you can know why I, Odin, the Eldest of the Gods, hung on the tree Ygdrassil nine days and nine nights, mine own spear transfixing me? I hung upon that windy tree that I might learn the wisdom that would give me power in the nine worlds. On the ninth night the Runes of Wisdom appeared before mine eyes, and slipping down from the tree I took them to myself.

"And I shall tell why my ravens fly to thee, carrying in their beaks scraps of leather. It is that thou mayst make for thyself a sandal; with that sandal on thou mayst put thy foot on the lower jaw of a mighty wolf and rend him. All the shoemakers of the earth throw on the ground scraps of the leather they use so that thou mayst be able to make the sandal for thy wolf-rending foot.

"And I have counseled the dwellers on earth to cut off the fingernails and the toenails of their dead, lest from those fingernails and toenails the Giants make for themselves the ship Naglfar in which they will sail from the North on the day of Ragnarök, the Twilight of the Gods.

"More, Vidar, I will tell to thee. I, living amongst men, have wed the daughter of a hero. My son shall live as a mortal amongst mortals. Sigi his name shall be. From him shall spring heroes who will fill Valhalla, my own hall in Asgard, with heroes against the day of our strife with the Giants and with Surtur of the Flaming Sword."

For long Odin stayed in that silent place communing with his silent son, with Vidar, who with his brother would live beyond the lives of the Dwellers of Asgard and who would bring into another day and another world the memory of the Æsir and the Vanir. For long Odin spoke with him, and then he went across the wilderness where the grass and the bushes grew and where that horse grazed in readiness for the sudden journey. He went toward the seashore where the Æsir and the Vanir were now gathered for the feast that old Ægir, the Giant King of the Sea, had offered them.

THOR AND LOKI IN THE GIANTS' CITY

ALL but a few of the Dwellers of Asgard had come to the feast offered by Ægir the Old, the Giant King of the Sea. Frigga, the queenly wife of Odin, was there, and Frey and Freya; Iduna, who guarded the Apples of Youth, and Bragi, her husband; Tyr, the great swordsman, and Niörd, the God of the Sea, Skadi, who wedded Niörd and whose hatred for Loki was fierce, and Sif, whose golden hair was once shorn off by Loki the mischievous. Thor and Loki were there. The Dwellers of Asgard, gathered together in the hall of Ægir, waited for Odin.

Before Odin came Loki made the company merry by the tales that he told in mockery of Thor. Loki long since had his lips unloosed from the thong that the Dwarf Brock had sewn them with. And Thor had forgotten the wrong that he had done to Sif. Loki had been with Thor in his wanderings through Jötunheim, and about these wanderings he now told mocking tales.

He told how he had seen Thor in his chariot of brass drawn by two goats go across Bifröst, the Rainbow Bridge. None of the Æsir or the Vanir knew on what adventure Thor was bent. But Loki followed him and Thor kept him in his company.

As they traveled on in the brass chariot drawn by the two goats, Thor told Loki of the adventure on which he was bent. He would go into Jötunheim, even into Utgard, the Giants' City, and he would try his strength against the Giants. He was not afraid of aught that might happen, for he carried Miölnir, his hammer, with him.

Their way was through Midgard, the World of Men. Once, as they were traveling on, night came upon them as they were hungry and in need of shelter. They saw a peasant's hut and they drove the chariot toward it. Unyoking the goats and leaving them standing in a hollow beside the chariot, the two, looking not like Dwellers in Asgard, but like men traveling through the country, knocked at the door of the hut and asked for food and shelter.

They could have shelter, the peasant and his wife told them, but they could not have food. There was little in that place, and what little there had been they had eaten for supper. The peasant showed them the inside of the hut: it was poor and bare, and there was nothing there to give anyone. In the morning, the peasant said, he would go down to the river and catch some fish for a meal.

"We can't wait until morning, we must eat now," said Thor, "and I think I can provide a good meal for us all." He went over to where his goats stood in the hollow beside the chariot of brass, and, striking them with his hammer, he left them lifeless on the ground. He skinned the goats then, and taking up the bones very carefully, he left them down on the skins. Skins and bones he lifted up and bringing them into the house he left them in a hole above the peasant's fireplace. "No one," said he in a commanding voice, "must touch the bones that I leave here."

Then he brought the meat into the house. Soon it was cooked and laid smoking on the table. The peasant and his wife and his son sat round the board with Thor and Loki. They had not eaten plentifully for many days, and now the man and the woman fed themselves well.

Thialfi was the name of the peasant's son. He was a growing lad and had an appetite that had not been satisfied for long. While the meat was on the table his father and mother had kept him going here and there, carrying water, putting fagots on the fire, and holding a blazing stick so that those at the table might see to eat. There was not much left for him when he was able to sit down, for Thor and Loki had great appetites, and the lad's father and mother had eaten to make up for days of want. So Thialfi got little out of that plentiful feast.

When the meal was finished they lay down on the benches. Thor, because he had made a long journey that day, slept very soundly. Thialfi lay down on a bench, too, but his thoughts were still upon the food. When all were asleep, he thought, he would take one of the bones that were in the skins above him, and break and gnaw it.

So in the dead of the night the lad stood up on the bench and took down the goatskins that Thor had left so carefully there. He took out a bone, broke it, and gnawed it for the marrow. Loki was awake and saw him do this, but he, relishing mischief as much as ever, did nothing to stay the lad.

He put the bone he had broken back in the skins and he left the skins back in the hole above the fireplace. Then he went to sleep on the bench.

In the morning, as soon as they were up, the first thing Thor did was to take the skins out of the hole. He carried them carefully out to the hollow where he had left the goats standing. He put each goatskin down with the bones in it. He struck each with his hammer, and the goats sprang up alive, horns and hoofs and all.

But one was not as he had been before. He limped badly. Thor examined the leg and found out that one bone was broken. In terrible anger he turned on the peasant, his wife, and his son. "A bone of this goat has been broken under your roof," he shouted. "For that I shall destroy your house and leave you all dead under it." Thialfi wept. Then he came forward and touched the knees of Thor. "I did not know what harm I did," he said. "I broke the bone."

Thor had his hammer lifted up to crush him into the earth. But he could not bring it down on the weeping boy. He let his hammer rest on the ground again. "You will have to do much service for me for having lamed my goat," he said. "Come with me."

And so the lad Thialfi went off with Thor and Loki. Thor took in his powerful hands the shafts of the chariot of brass and he dragged it into a lonely mountain hollow where neither men nor Giants came. And they left the goats in a great, empty forest to stay resting there until Thor called to them again.

Thor and Loki and the lad Thialfi went across from Midgard into Jötunheim. Because of Miölnir, the great hammer that he carried, Thor felt safe in the Realm of the Giants. And Loki, who trusted in his own cunning, felt safe, too. The lad Thialfi trusted in Thor so much that he had no fear. They were long in making the journey, and while they were traveling Thor and Loki trained Thialfi to be a quick and a strong lad.

One day they came out on a moor. All day they crossed it, and at night it still stretched far before them. A great wind was blowing, night was falling, and they saw no shelter near. In the dusk they saw a shape that looked to be a mountain and they went toward it, hoping to find some shelter in a cave.

Then Loki saw a lower shape that looked as if it might be a shelter. They walked around it, Loki and Thor and the lad Thialfi. It was a house, but a house most oddly shaped. The entrance was a long, wide hall that had no doorway. When they entered this hall they found five long and narrow chambers running off it. "It is an odd place, but it is the best shelter we can get," Loki said. "You and

I, Thor, will take the two longest rooms, and the lad Thialfi can take one of the little rooms."

They entered their chambers and they lay down to sleep. But from the mountain outside there came a noise that was like moaning forests and falling cataracts. The chamber where each one slept was shaken by the noise. Neither Thor nor Loki nor the lad Thialfi slept that night.

In the morning they left the five-chambered house and turned their faces toward the mountain. It was not a mountain at all, but a Giant. He was lying on the ground when they saw him, but just then he rolled over and sat up. "Little men, little men," he shouted to them, "have you passed by a glove of mine on your way?" He stood up and looked all around him. "Ho, I see my glove now," he said. Thor and Loki and the lad Thialfi stood still as the Giant came toward them. He leaned over and picked up the five-roomed shelter they had slept in. He put it on his hand. It was really his glove!

Thor gripped his hammer, and Loki and the lad Thialfi stood behind him. But the Giant seemed good-humored enough. "Where might ye be bound for, little men?" said he.

"To Utgard in Jötunheim," Thor replied boldly.

"Oh, to that place," said the Giant. "Come, then, I shall be with ye so far. You can call me Skyrmir."

"Can you give us breakfast?" said Thor. He spoke crossly, for he did not want it to appear that there was any reason to be afraid of the Giant.

"I can give you breakfast," said Skyrmir, "but I don't

want to stop to eat now. We'll sit down as soon as I have an appetite. Come along now. Here is my wallet to carry. It has my provisions in it."

He gave Thor his wallet. Thor put it on his back and put Thialfi sitting upon it. On and on the Giant strode and Thor and Loki were barely able to keep up with him. It was midday before he showed any signs of halting to take breakfast.

They came to an enormous tree. Under it Skyrmir sat down. "I'll sleep before I eat," he said, "but you can open my wallet, my little men, and make your meal out of it." Saying this, he stretched himself out, and in a few minutes Thor and Loki and the lad Thialfi heard the same sounds as kept them awake the night before, sounds that were like forests moaning and cataracts falling. It was Skyrmir's snoring.

Thor and Loki and the lad Thialfi were too hungry now to be disturbed by these tremendous noises. Thor tried to open the wallet, but he found it was not easy to undo the knots. Then Loki tried to open it. In spite of all Loki's cunning he could not undo the knots. Then Thor took the wallet from him and tried to break the knots by main strength. Not even Thor's strength could break them. He threw the wallet down in his rage.

The snoring of Skyrmir became louder and louder. Thor stood up in his rage. He grasped Miölnir and flung it at the head of the sleeping Giant.

The hammer struck him on the head. But Skyrmir only stirred in his sleep. "Did a leaf fall on my head?" he said.

He turned round on the other side and went to sleep again. The hammer came back to Thor's hand. As soon as Skyrmir snored he flung it again, aiming at the Giant's forehead. It struck there. The Giant opened his eyes. "Has an acorn fallen on my forehead?" he said.

Again he went to sleep. But now Thor, terribly roused, stood over his head with the hammer held in his hands. He struck him on the forehead. It was the greatest blow that Thor had ever dealt.

"A bird is pecking at my forehead — there is no chance to sleep here," said Skyrmir, sitting up. "And you, little men, did you have breakfast yet? Toss over my wallet to me and I shall give you some provision." The lad Thialfi brought him the wallet. Skyrmir opened it, took out his provisions, and gave a share to Thor and Loki and the lad Thialfi. Thor would not take provision from him, but Loki and the lad Thialfi took it and ate. When the meal was finished Skyrmir rose up and said, "Time for us to be going toward Utgard."

As they went on their way Skyrmir talked to Loki. "I always feel very small when I go into Utgard," he said. "You see, I'm such a small and a weak fellow and the folk who live there are so big and powerful. But you and your friends will be welcomed in Utgard. They will be sure to make little pets of you."

And then he left them and they went into Utgard, the City of the Giants. Giants were going up and down in the streets. They were not so huge as Skyrmir would have them believe, Loki noticed.

Utgard was the Asgard of the Giants. But in its buildings there was not a line of the beauty that there was in the palaces of the Gods, Gladsheim and Breidablik or Fensalir. Huge but shapeless the buildings arose, like mountains or icebergs. O beautiful Asgard with the dome above it of the deepest blue! Asgard with the clouds around it heaped up like mountains of diamonds! Asgard with its Rainbow Bridge and its glittering gates! O beautiful Asgard, could it be indeed that these Giants would one day overthrow you?

Thor and Loki with the lad Thialfi went to the palace of the King. The hammer that Thor gripped would, they knew, make them safe even there. They passed between rows of Giant guards and came to the King's seat. "We know you, Thor and Loki," said the Giant King, "and we know that Thor has come to Utgard to try his strength against the Giants. We shall have a contest tomorrow. Today there are sports for our boys. If your young servant should like to try his swiftness against our youths, let him enter the race today."

Now Thialfi was the best runner in Midgard and all the time he had been with them Loki and Thor had trained him in quickness. And so Thialfi was not fearful of racing against the Giants' youths.

The King called on one named Hugi and placed him against Thialfi. The pair started together. Thialfi sped off. Loki and Thor watched the race anxiously, for they thought it would be well for them if they had a triumph over the dwellers in Utgard in the first contest. But they saw Hugi leave Thialfi behind. They saw the Giant youth reach the winning post, circle round it, and come back to the starting place before Thialfi had reached the end of the course.

Thialfi, who did not know how it was that he had been beaten, asked that he be let run the race with Hugi again. The pair started off once more, and this time it did not seem to Thor and Loki that Hugi had left the starting place at all — he was back there almost as soon as the race had started.

They came back from the racing ground to the palace. The Giant King and his friends with Thor and Loki sat down to the supper table. "Tomorrow," said the King, "we shall have our great contest when Asa Thor will show us his power. Have you of Asgard ever heard of one who would enter a contest in eating? We might have a contest in eating at this supper board if we could get one who would match himself with Logi here. He can eat more than anyone in Jötunheim."

"And I," said Loki, "can eat more than any two in Jötunheim. I will match myself against your Logi."

"Good!" said the Giant King. And all the Giants present said, "Good! This will be a sight worth seeing."

Then they put scores of plates along one side of the table, each plate filled with meat. Loki began at one end and Logi began at the other. They started to eat, moving toward each other as each cleared a plate. Plate after plate was emptied, and Thor standing by with the Giants was amazed to see how much Loki ate. But Logi on the other side was leaving plate after plate emptied. At last the two stood together with scores of plates on each side of them. "He has not defeated me," cried Loki. "I have cleared as many plates as your champion, O King of the Giants."

"But you have not cleared them so well," said the King.

"Loki has eaten all the meat that was upon them," said Thor.

"But Logi has eaten the bones with the meat," said the Giant King. "Look and see if it be not so."

Thor went to the plates. Where Loki had eaten, the bones were left on the plates. Where Logi had eaten, nothing was left: bones as well as meat were consumed, and all the plates were left bare.

"We are beaten," said Thor to Loki.

"Tomorrow, Thor," said Loki, "you must show all your strength or the Giants will cease to dread the might of the Dwellers in Asgard."

"Be not afraid," said Thor. "No one in Jötunheim will triumph over me."

The next day Thor and Loki came into the great hall of Utgard. The Giant King was there with a throng of his friends. Thor marched into the hall with Miölnir, his great hammer, in his hands. "Our young men have been drinking out of this horn," said the King, "and they want to know if you, Asa Thor, would drink out of it a morning draught. But I must tell you that they think that no one of the Æsir could empty the horn at one draught."

"Give it to me," said Thor. "There is no horn you can hand me that I cannot empty at a draught."

A great horn, brimmed and flowing, was brought over to him. Handing Miölnir to Loki and bidding him stand so that he might keep the hammer in sight, Thor raised the horn to his mouth. He drank and drank. He felt sure there was not a drop left in the horn as he laid it on the ground. "There," he gasped, "your Giant horn is drained."

The Giants looked within the horn and laughed. "Drained, Asa Thor!" said the Giant King. "Look into the horn again. You have hardly drunk below the brim."

And Thor looked into it and saw that the horn was not half emptied. In a mighty rage he lifted it to his lips again. He drank and drank and drank. Then, satisfied that he had emptied it to the bottom, he left the horn on the ground and walked over to the other side of the hall.

"Thor thinks he has drained the horn," said one of the Giants, lifting it up. "But see, friends, what remains in it."

Thor strode back and looked again into the horn. It was still half filled. He turned round to see that all the Giants were laughing at him.

"Asa Thor, Asa Thor," said the Giant King, "we know not how you are going to deal with us in the next feat, but you certainly are not able to drink against the Giants."

Said Thor: "I can lift up and set down any being in your hall."

As he said this a great iron-colored cat bounded into the hall and stood before Thor, her back arched and her fur bristling.

"Then lift the cat off the ground," said the Giant King.

Thor strode to the cat, determined to lift her up and

fling her amongst the mocking Giants. He put his hands to the cat, but he could not raise her. Up, up went Thor's arms, up, up, as high as they could go. The cat's arched back went up to the roof, but her feet were never taken off the ground. And as he heaved and heaved with all his might he heard the laughter of the Giants all round him.

He turned away, his eyes flaming with anger. "I am not wont to try to lift cats," he said. "Bring me one to wrestle with, and I swear you shall see me overthrow him."

"Here is one for you to wrestle with, Asa Thor," said the King. Thor looked round and saw an old woman hobbling toward him. She was blear-eyed and toothless. "This is Ellie, my ancient nurse," said the Giant King. "She is the one we would have you wrestle with."

"Thor does not wrestle with old women. I will lay my hands on your tallest Giants instead."

"Ellie has come where you are," said the Giant King. "Now it is she who will lay hands upon you."

The old woman hobbled toward Thor, her eyes gleaming under her falling fringes of gray hair. Thor stood, unable to move as the hag came toward him. She laid her hands upon his arms. Her feet began to trip at his. He tried to cast her from him. Then he found that her feet and her hands were as strong against his as bands and stakes of iron.

Then began a wrestling match in earnest between Thor and the ancient crone Ellie. Round and round the hall they wrestled, and Thor was not able to bend the old woman backward nor sideways. Instead he became less and less able under her terrible grasp. She forced him down, down, and at last he could only save himself from being left prone on the ground by throwing himself down on one knee and holding the hag by the shoulders. She tried to force him down on the ground, but she could not do that. Then she broke from him, hobbled to the door and went out of the hall.

Thor rose up and took the hammer from Loki's hands. Without a word he went out of the hall and along the ways and toward the gate of the Giants' City. He spoke no word to Loki nor to the lad Thialfi who went with him for the seven weeks that they journeyed through Jötunheim.

HOW THOR AND LOKI BEFOOLED THRYM THE GIANT

LOKI told another tale about Thor — about Thor and Thrym, a stupid Giant who had cunning streaks in him. Loki and Thor had been in this Giant's house. He had made a feast for them and Thor had been unwatchful.

Then when they were far from Jötunheim Thor missed Miölnir, missed the hammer that was the defence of Asgard and the help of the Gods. He could not remember how or where he had mislaid it. Loki's thoughts went toward Thrym, that stupid Giant who yet had cunning streaks in him. Thor, who had lost the hammer that he had sworn never to let out of his sight, did not know what to do.

But Loki thought it would be worth while to see if Thrym knew anything about it. He went first to Asgard.

He hurried across the Rainbow Bridge and passed Heimdall without speaking to him. To none of the Dwellers in Asgard whom he met did he dare relate the tidings of Thor's loss. He spoke to none until he came to Frigga's palace.

To Frigga he said, "You must lend me your falcon dress until I fly to Thrym's dwelling and find out if he knows where Miölnir is."

"If every feather was silver I would give it to you to go on such an errand," Frigga said.

So Loki put on the falcon dress and flew to Jötunheim and came near Thrym's dwelling. He found the Giant upon a hillside putting golden and silver collars upon the necks of his hounds. Loki in the plumage of a falcon perched on the rock above him, watching the Giant with falcon eyes.

And while he was there he heard the Giant speak boastful words. "I put collars of silver and gold on you now, my hounds," said he, "but soon we Giants will have the gold of Asgard to deck our hounds and our steeds, yea, even the necklace of Freya to put upon you, the best of my hounds. For Miölnir, the defence of Asgard, is in Thrym's holding."

Then Loki spoke to him. "Yea, we know that Miölnir is in thy possession, O Thrym," said he, "but know thou that the eyes of the watchful Gods are upon thee."

"Ha, Loki, Shape-changer," said Thrym, "you are there! But all your watching will not help you to find Miölnir.

I have buried Thor's hammer eight miles deep in the earth. Find it if you can. It is below the caves of the Dwarfs."

"It is useless for us to search for Thor's hammer," said Loki; "eh, Thrym?"

"It is useless for you to search for it," said the Giant sulkily.

"But what a recompense you would gain if you restored Thor's hammer to the Dwellers in Asgard," Loki said.

"No, cunning Loki, I will never restore it, not for any recompense," said Thrym.

"Yet bethink thee, Thrym," said Loki. "Is there nought in Asgard you would like to own? No treasure, no possession? Odin's ring or Frey's ship, Skidbladnir?"

"No, no," said Thrym. "Only one thing could the Dwellers in Asgard offer me that I would take in exchange for Miölnir, Thor's hammer."

"And what would that be, Thrym?" said Loki, flying toward him.

"She whom many Giants have striven to gain — Freya, for my wife," said Thrym.

Loki watched Thrym for long with his falcon eyes. He saw that the Giant would not alter his demand. "I will tell the Dwellers in Asgard of your demand," he said at last, and he flew away.

Loki knew that the Dwellers in Asgard would never let Freya be taken from them to become the wife of Thrym, the stupidest of the Giants. He flew back.

By this time all the Dwellers in Asgard had heard of the

loss of Miölnir, the help of the Gods. Heimdall shouted to him as he crossed the Rainbow Bridge to ask what tidings he brought back. But Loki did not stop to speak to the Warden of the Bridge but went straight to the hall where the Gods sat in Council.

To the Æsir and the Vanir he told Thrym's demand. None would agree to let the beautiful Freya go live in Jötunheim as a wife to the stupidest of the Giants. All in the Council were cast down. The Gods would never again be able to help mortal men, for now that Miölnir was in the Giants' hands all their strength would have to be used in the defence of Asgard.

So they sat in the Council with looks downcast. But cunning Loki said, "I have thought of a trick that may win back the hammer from stupid Thrym. Let us pretend to send Freya to Jötunheim as a bride for him. But let one of the Gods go in Freya's veil and dress."

"Which of the Gods would bring himself to do so shameful a thing?" said those in the Council.

"Oh, he who lost the hammer, Thor, should be prepared to do as much to win it back," said Loki.

"Thor, Thor! Let Thor win back the hammer from Thrym by Loki's trick," said the Æsir and the Vanir. They left it to Loki to arrange how Thor should go to Jötunheim as a bride for Thrym.

Loki left the Council of the Gods and came to where he had left Thor. "There is but one way to win the hammer back, Thor," he said, "and the Gods in Council have decreed that you shall take it."

"What is the way?" said Thor. "But no matter what it is, tell me of it and I shall do as thou dost say."

"Then," said laughing Loki, "I am to take you to Jötunheim as a bride for Thrym. Thou art to go in bridal dress and veil, in Freya's veil and bridal dress."

"What! I dress in woman's garb?" shouted Thor.

"Yea, Thor, and wear a veil over your head and a garland of flowers upon it."

"I — I wear a garland of flowers?"

"And rings upon thy fingers. And a bunch of housekeeper's keys in thy girdle."

"Cease thy mockery, Loki," said Thor roughly, "or I shall shake thee."

"It is no mockery. Thou wilt have to do this to win Miölnir back for the defence of Asgard. Thrym will take no other recompense than Freya. I would mock him by bringing thee to him in Freya's veil and dress. When thou art in his hall and he asks thee to join hands with him, say thou wilt not until he puts Miölnir into thy hands. Then when thy mighty hammer is in thy holding thou canst deal with him and with all in his hall. And I shall be with thee as thy bridesmaid! O sweet, sweet maiden Thor!"

"Loki," said Thor, "thou didst devise all this to mock me. I in a bridal dress! I with a bride's veil upon me! The Dwellers in Asgard will never cease to laugh at me."

"Yea," said Loki, "but there will never be laughter again in Asgard unless thou art able to bring back the hammer that thine unwatchfulness lost."

"True," said Thor unhappily, "and is this, thinkst

thou, Loki, the only way to win back Miölnir from Thrym?"

"It is the only way, O Thor," said the cunning Loki.

So Thor and Loki set out for Jötunheim and the dwelling of Thrym. A messenger had gone before them to tell Thrym that Freya was coming with her bridesmaid; that the wedding-feast was to be prepared and the guests gathered and that Miölnir was to be at hand so that it might be given over to the Dwellers in Asgard. Thrym and his Giant mother hastened to have everything in readiness.

Thor and Loki came to the Giant's house in the dress of a bride and a bridesmaid. A veil was over Thor's head hiding his beard and his fierce eyes. A red-embroidered robe he wore and at his side hung a girdle of housekeeper's keys. Loki was veiled, too. The hall of Thrym's great house was swept and garnished and great tables were laid for the feast. And Thrym's mother was going from one guest to another, vaunting that her son was getting one of the beauteous Dwellers in Asgard for his bride, Freya, whom so many of the Giants had tried to win.

When Thor and Loki stepped across the threshold Thrym went to welcome them. He wanted to raise the veil of his bride and give her a kiss. Loki quickly laid his hand on the Giant's shoulder.

"Forbear," he whispered. "Do not raise her veil. We Dwellers in Asgard are reserved and bashful. Freya would be much offended to be kissed before this company."

"Aye, aye," said Thrym's old mother. "Do not raise thy bride's veil, son. These Dwellers in Asgard are more refined in their ways than we, the Giants." Then the old woman took Thor by the hand and led him to the table.

The size and the girth of the bride did not surprise the huge Giants who were in the wedding company. They stared at Thor and Loki, but they could see nothing of their faces and little of their forms because of their veils.

Thor sat at the table with Thrym on one side of him and Loki on the other. Then the feast began. Thor, not noticing that what he did was unbecoming to a refined maiden, ate eight salmon right away. Loki nudged him and pressed his foot, but he did not heed Loki. After the salmon he ate a whole ox.

"These maids of Asgard," said the Giants to each other, "they may be refined, as Thrym's mother says, but their appetites are lusty enough."

"No wonder she eats, poor thing," said Loki to Thrym. "It is eight days since we left Asgard. And Freya never ate upon the way, so anxious was she to see Thrym and to come to his house."

"Poor darling, poor darling," said the Giant. "What she has eaten is little after all."

Thor nodded his head toward the mead vat. Thrym ordered his servants to bring a measure to his bride. The servants were kept coming with measures to Thor. While the Giants watched, and while Loki nudged and nodded, he drank three barrels of mead.

"Oh," said the Giants to Thrym's mother, "we are not so sorry that we failed to win a bride from Asgard."

And now a piece of the veil slipped aside and Thor's

eyes were seen for an instant. "Oh, how does it come that Freya has such glaring eyes?" said Thrym.

"Poor thing, poor thing," said Loki, "no wonder her eyes are glaring and staring. She has not slept for eight nights, so anxious was she to come to you and to your house, Thrym. But now the time has come for you to join hands with your bride. First, put into her hands the hammer Miölnir that she may know the great recompense that the Giants have given for her coming."

Then Thrym, the stupidest of the Giants, rose up and brought Miölnir, the defence of Asgard, into the feasting hall. Thor could hardly restrain himself from springing up and seizing it from the Giant. But Loki was able to keep him still. Thrym brought over the hammer and put the handle into the hands of her whom he thought was his bride. Thor's hands closed on his hammer. Instantly he stood up. The veil fell off him. His countenance and his blazing eyes were seen by all. He struck one blow on the wall of the house. Down it crashed. Then Thor went striding out of the ruin with Loki beside him, while within the Giants bellowed as the roof and walls fell down on them. And so was Miölnir, the defence of Asgard, lost and won back.

AEGIR'S FEAST:
HOW THOR TRIUMPHED

THE time between midday and evening wore on while the Æsir and the Vanir gathered for the feast in old Ægir's hall listened to the stories that Loki told in mockery of Thor. The night came, but no banquet was made ready for the Dwellers in Asgard. They called to Ægir's two underservants, Fimaffenger and Elder, and they bade them bring them a supper. Slight was what they got, but they went to bed saying, "Great must be the preparations that old Ægir is making to feast us tomorrow."

The morrow came and the midday of the morrow, and still the Dwellers in Asgard saw no preparations being made for the banquet. Then Frey rose up and went to seek old Ægir, the Giant King of the Sea. He found him sitting with bowed head in his inner hall. "Ho, Ægir," he said, "what of the banquet that you have offered to the Dwellers in Asgard?"

Old Ægir mumbled and pulled at his beard. At last he looked his guest in the face and told why the banquet was not being made ready. The mead for the feast was not yet brewed. And there was little chance of being able to brew mead that would do for all, for Ægir's hall was lacking a mead kettle that would contain enough.

When the Æsir and the Vanir heard this they were sorely disappointed. Who now, outside of Asgard, would give them a feast? Ægir was the only one of the Giants who was friendly to them, and Ægir could not give them full entertainment.

Then a Giant youth who was there spoke up and said, "My kinsman, the Giant Hrymer, has a mead kettle that is a mile wide. If we could bring Hrymer's kettle here, what a feast we might have!"

"One of us can go for that kettle," Frey said.

"Ah, but Hrymer's dwelling is beyond the deepest forest and behind the highest mountain," the Giant youth said, "and Hrymer himself is a rough and a churlish one to call on."

"Still, one of us should go," Frey said.

"I will go to Hrymer's dwelling," said Thor, standing up. "I will go to Hrymer's dwelling and get the mile-wide kettle from him by force or cunning." He had been sitting subdued under the mocking tales that Loki told of him and he was pleased with this chance to make his prowess plain to the Æsir and the Vanir. He buckled on the belt that doubled his strength. He drew on the iron gloves that enabled him to grasp Miölnir. He took his hammer in his hands, and he signed to the Giant youth to come with him and be his guide.

The Æsir and the Vanir applauded Thor as he stepped out of old Ægir's hall. But Loki, mischievous Loki, threw a gibe after him. "Do not let the hammer out of your hands this time, bride of Thrym," he shouted.

Thor, with the Giant youth to guide him, went through the deepest forest and over the highest mountain. He came at last to the Giant's dwelling. On a hillock before Hrymer's house was a dreadful warden; a Giant crone she was, with heads a-many growing out of her shoulders. She was squatting down on her ankles, and her heads, growing in bunches, were looking in different directions. As Thor and the Giant youth came near screams and yelps came from all her heads. Thor grasped his hammer and would have flung it at her if a Giant woman, making a sign of peace, had not come to the door of the dwelling. The youthful Giant who was with Thor greeted her as his mother.

"Son, come within," said she, "and you may bring your fellow farer with you."

The Giant crone — she was Hrymer's grandmother — kept up her screaming and yelping. But Thor went past her and into the Giant's dwelling.

When she saw that it was one of the Dwellers in Asgard who had come with her son the Giant woman grew fearful for them both. "Hrymer," she said, "will be in a rage to find one of the Æsir under his roof. He will strive to slay you."

"It is not likely he will succeed," Thor said, grasping Miölnir, the hammer that all the Giant race knew of and dreaded.

"Hide from him," said the Giant woman. "He may injure my son in his rage to find you here."

"I am not wont to hide from the Giants," Thor said.

"Hide only for a little while! Hide until Hrymer has eaten," the Giant woman pleaded. "He comes back from the chase in a stormy temper. After he has eaten he is easier to deal with. Hide until he has finished supper."

Thor at last agreed to do this. He and the Giant youth hid behind a pillar in the hall. They were barely hidden when they heard the clatter of the Giant's steps as he came through the courtyard. He came to the door. His beard was like a frozen forest around his mouth. And he dragged along with him a wild bull that he had captured in the chase. So proud was he of his capture that he dragged it into the hall.

"I have taken alive," he shouted, "the bull with the mightiest head and horns. 'Heaven-breaking' this bull is called. No Giant but me could capture it." He tied the bull to the post of the door and then his eyes went toward the pillar behind which Thor and the Giant youth were hiding. The pillar split up its whole length at that look from Hrymer's eyes. He came nearer. The pillar of stone broke across. It fell with the crossbeam it supported and all the kettles and cauldrons that were hanging on the beam came down with a terrible rattle.

Then Thor stepped out and faced the wrathful Giant. "It is I who am here, friend Hrymer," he said, his hands resting on his hammer.

Then Hrymer, who knew Thor and knew the force of Thor's hammer, drew back. "Now that you are in my house, Asa Thor," he said, "I will not quarrel with you. Make supper ready for Asa Thor and your son and myself," said he to the Giant woman.

A plentiful supper was spread and Hrymer and Thor and the Giant youth sat down to three whole roast oxen. Thor ate the whole of one ox. Hrymer, who had eaten nearly two himself, leaving only small cuts for his wife and his youthful kinsman, grumbled at Thor's appetite. "You'll clear my fields, Asa Thor," he said, "if you stay long with me."

"Do not grumble, Hrymer," Thor said. "Tomorrow I'll go fishing and I'll bring you back the weight of what I ate."

"Then instead of hunting I'll go fishing with you tomorrow, Asa Thor," said Hrymer. "And don't be frightened if I take you out on a rough sea."

Hrymer was first out of bed the next morning. He came with the pole and the ropes in his hand to where Thor was sleeping. "Time to start earning your meal, Asa Thor," said he.

Thor got out of bed, and when they were both in the courtyard the Giant said, "You'll have to provide a bait for yourself. Mind that you take a bait large enough. It is not where the little fishes are, the place where I'm going to take you. If you never saw monsters before you'll see them now. I'm glad, Asa Thor, that you spoke of going fishing."

"Will this bait be big enough?" said Thor, laying his hands on the horns of the bull that Hrymer had captured and brought home, the bull with the mighty head of horns that was called "Heaven-breaking." "Will this bait be big enough, do you think?"

"Yes, if you're big enough to handle it," said the Giant.

Thor said nothing, but he struck the bull full in the middle of the forehead with his fist. The great creature fell down dead. Thor then twisted the bull's head off. "I have my bait and I'm ready to go with you, Hrymer," he said.

Hrymer had turned away to hide the rage he was in at seeing Thor do such a feat. He walked down to the boat without speaking. "You may row for the first few strokes," said Hrymer, when they were in the boat, "but when we come to where the ocean is rough, why I'll take the oars from you."

Without saying a word Thor made a few strokes that took the boat out into the middle of the ocean. Hrymer was in a rage to think that he could not show himself greater than Thor. He let out his line and began to fish. Soon he felt something huge on his hook. The boat rocked and rocked till Thor steadied it. Then Hrymer drew into the boat the largest whale that was in these seas.

"Good fishing," said Thor, as he put his own bait on the line.

"It's something for you to tell the Æsir," said Hrymer. "I thought as you were here I'd show you something bigger than salmon-fishing."

"I'll try my luck now," said Thor.

He threw out a line that had at the end of it the mighty-horned head of the great bull. Down, down the head went. It passed where the whales swim, and the whales were afraid to gulp at the mighty horns. Down, down it went till it came near where the monster serpent that coils itself round the world abides. It reared its head up from its serpent coils as Thor's bait came down through the depths of the ocean. It gulped at the head and drew it into its gullet. There the great hook stuck. Terribly surprised was the serpent monster. It lashed the ocean into a fury. But still the hook stayed. Then it strove to draw down to the depths of the ocean the boat of those who had hooked it. Thor put his legs across the boat and stretched them till they touched the bottom bed of the ocean. On the bottom bed of the ocean Thor stood and he pulled and he pulled on his line. The serpent monster lashed the ocean into fiercer and fiercer storms and all the world's ships were hurled against each other and wrecked and tossed. But it had to loosen coil after coil of the coils it makes around the world. Thor pulled and pulled. Then the terrible head of the serpent monster appeared above the waters. It reared over the boat that Hrymer sat in and that Thor straddled across. Thor dropped the line and took up Miölnir, his mighty hammer. He raised it to strike the head of the serpent monster whose coils go round the world. But Hrymer would not have that happen. Rather than have Thor pass him by such a feat he cut the line, and the head of the serpent monster sank back into the sea. Thor's hammer was raised. He hurled it, hurled that hammer that always came back to his hand. It followed the sinking head through fathom after fathom of the ocean depth. It struck the serpent monster a blow, but not such a deadly blow as would have been struck if the water had not come between. A bellow of pain came up from the depths of the ocean, such a bellow of pain that all in Jötunheim were affrighted.

"This surely is something to tell the Æsir of," said Thor, "something to make them forget Loki's mockeries."

Without speaking Hrymer turned the boat and rowed toward the shore, dragging the whale in the wake. He was in such a rage to think that one of the Æsir had done a feat surpassing his that he would not speak. At supper, too, he remained silent, but Thor talked for two, boasting loudly of his triumph over the monster serpent.

"No doubt you think yourself very powerful, Asa Thor," Hrymer said at last. "Well, do you think you are powerful enough to break the cup that is before you?"

Thor took up the cup and with a laugh he hurled it against the stone pillar of the house. The cup fell down on the floor without a crack or a dint in it. But the pillar was shattered with the blow.

The Giant laughed. "So feeble are the folk of Asgard!" he said.

Thor took up the cup again and flung it with greater

force against the stone pillar. And again the cup fell to the ground without a crack or a dint.

Then he heard the woman who was the mother of the Giant youth sing softly, as she plied her wheel behind him:

> Not at the pillar of the stead,
> But at Hrymer's massy head:
> When you next the goblet throw,
> Let his head receive the blow.

Thor took the cup up again. He flung it, not at the pillar this time, but at Hrymer's head. It struck the Giant full on the forehead and fell down on the floor in pieces. And Hrymer's head was left without a dint or a crack.

"Ha, so you can break a cup, but can you lift up my mile-wide kettle?" cried the Giant.

"Show me where your mile-wide kettle is and I shall try to lift it," cried Thor.

The Giant took up the flooring and showed him the mile-wide kettle down in the cellar. Thor stooped down and took the kettle by the brim. He lifted it slowly as if with a mighty effort.

"You can lift, but can you carry it?" said the Giant.

"I will try to do that," said Thor. He lifted the kettle up and placed it on his head. He strode to the door and out of the house before the Giant could lay hands on him. Then when he was outside he started to run. He was across the mountain before he looked behind him. He heard a yelping and a screaming and he saw the Giant crone with the bunch of heads running, running after him. Up hill and down dale Thor raced, the mile-wide kettle on his head and the Giant crone in chase of him. Through the deep forest he ran and over the high mountain, but still Bunch-of-Heads kept him in chase. But at last, jumping over a lake, she fell in and Thor was free of his pursuer.

And so back to the Æsir and the Vanir Thor came in triumph, carrying on his head the mile-wide kettle. And those of the Æsir and the Vanir who had laughed most at Loki's mockeries rose up and cheered for him as he came in. The mead was brewed, the feast was spread, and the greatest banquet that ever the Kings of the Giants gave to the Dwellers in Asgard was eaten in gladness.

A strange and silent figure sat at the banquet. It was the figure of a Giant and no one knew who he was nor where he had come from. But when the banquet was ended Odin, the Eldest of the Gods, turned toward this figure and said, "O Skyrmir, Giant King of Utgard, rise up now and tell Thor of all you practiced upon him when he and Loki came to your City."

Then the stranger at the banquet stood up, and Thor and Loki saw he was the Giant King in whose halls they had had the contests. Skyrmir turned toward them and said:

"O Thor and O Loki, I will reveal to you now the deceits I practiced on you both. It was I whom ye met on the moorland on the day before ye came into Utgard. I gave you my name as Skyrmir and I did all I might do to prevent your entering our City, for the Giants dreaded a contest of strength with Asa Thor. Now hear me, O Thor. The wallet I gave for you to take provisions out of was tied with magic knots. No one could undo them by strength or cleverness. And while you were striving to undo them I placed a mountain of rock between myself and you. The hammer blows, which as you thought struck me, struck the mountain and made great clefts and gaps in it. When I knew the strength of your tremendous blows I was more and more in dread of your coming into our City.

"I saw you would have to be deceived by magic. Your lad Thialfi was the one whom I first deceived. For it was not a Giant youth who raced against him, but Thought itself. And even you, O Loki, I deceived. For when you tried to make yourself out the greatest of eaters I pitted against you, not a Giant, but Fire that devours everything.

"You, Thor, were deceived in all the contests. After you had taken the drinking horn in your hands we were all affrighted to see how much you were able to gulp down. For the end of that horn was in the sea, and Ægir, who is here, can tell you that after you had drunk from it, the level of the sea went down.

"The cat whom you strove to lift was Nidhögg, the dragon that gnaws at the roots of Ygdrassil, the Tree of Trees. Truly we were terrified when we saw that you made Nidhögg budge. When you made the back of the cat reach the roof of our palace we said to ourselves, 'Thor is the mightiest of all the beings we have known.'

"Lastly you strove with the hag Ellie. Her strength seemed marvelous to you, and you thought yourself disgraced because you could not throw her. But know, Thor, that Ellie whom you wrestled with was Old Age herself. We were terrified again to see that she who can overthrow all was not able to force you prone upon the ground."

So Skyrmir spoke and then left the hall. And once more the Æsir and the Vanir stood up and cheered for Thor, the strongest of all who guarded Asgard.

THE DWARF'S HOARD, AND THE
CURSE THAT IT BROUGHT

NOW old Ægir's feast was over and all the Æsir and the Vanir made ready for their return to Asgard. Two only went on another way — Odin, the Eldest of the Gods, and Loki the Mischievous.

Loki and Odin laid aside all that they had kept of the divine power and the divine strength. They were going into the World of Men, and they would be as men merely. Together they went through Midgard, mingling with men of all sorts, kings and farmers, outlaws and true men, warriors and householders, thralls and councillors, courteous men and men who were ill-mannered. One day they came to the bank of a mighty river and there they rested, listening to the beat of iron upon iron in a place near by.

Presently, on a rock in the middle of the river, they saw

an otter come. The otter went into the water and came back to the rock with a catch of salmon. He devoured it there. Then Odin saw Loki do a senseless and an evil thing. Taking up a great stone he flung it at the otter. The stone struck the beast on the skull and knocked him over dead.

"Loki, Loki, why hast thou done a thing so senseless and so evil?" Odin said. Loki only laughed. He swam across the water and came back with the creature of the river. "Why didst thou take the life of the beast?" Odin said.

"The mischief in me made me do it," said Loki. He drew out his knife and ripping the otter up he began to flay him. When the skin was off the beast he folded it up and stuck it in his belt. Then Odin and he left that place by the river.

They came to a house with two smithies beside it, and from the smithies came the sound of iron beating upon iron. They went within the house and they asked that they might eat there and rest themselves.

An old man who was cooking fish over a fire pointed out a bench to them. "Rest there," said he, "and when the fish is cooked I will give you something good to eat. My son is a fine fisher and he brings me salmon of the best."

Odin and Loki sat on the bench and the old man went on with his cooking. "My name is Hreidmar," he said, "and I have two sons who work in the smithies without. I have a third son also. It is he who does the fishing for us. And who may ye be, O wayfaring men?"

Loki and Odin gave names to Hreidmar that were not

the names by which they were known in Asgard or on Midgard. Hreidmar served fish to them and they ate. "And what adventures have ye met upon your travels?" Hreidmar asked. "Few folk come this way to tell me of happenings."

"I killed an otter with a cast of a stone," Loki said with a laugh.

"You killed an otter!" Hreidmar cried. "Where did you kill one?"

"Where I killed him is of no import to you, old man," said Loki. "His skin is a good one, however. I have it at my belt."

Hreidmar snatched the skin out of Loki's belt. As soon as he held the skin before his eyes he shrieked out, "Fafnir, Regin, my sons, come here and bring the thralls of your smithies. Come, come, come!"

"Why dost thou make such an outcry, old man?" said Odin.

"Ye have slain my son Otter," shrieked the old man. "This in my hands is the skin of my son."

As Hreidmar said this two young men bearing the forehammers of the smithies came in followed by the thralls. "Strike these men dead with your forehammers, O Fafnir, O Regin," their father cried. "Otter, who used to stay in the river, and whom I changed by enchantment into a river beast that he might fish for me, has been slain by these men."

"Peace," said Odin. "We have slain thy son, it would seem, but it was unwittingly that we did the deed. We will give a recompense for the death of thy son."

"What recompense will ye give?" said Hreidmar, looking at Odin with eyes that were small and sharp.

Then did Odin, the Eldest of the Gods, say a word that was unworthy of his wisdom and his power. He might have said, "I will bring thee a draught of Mimir's well water as a recompense for thy son's death." But instead of thinking of wisdom, Odin All-Father thought of gold. "Set a price on the life of thy son and we will pay that price in gold," he said.

"Maybe ye are great kings traveling through the world," Hreidmar said. "If ye are ye will have to find gold that will cover every hair upon the skin of him whom ye have killed."

Then did Odin, his mind being fixed upon the gold, think upon a certain treasure, a treasure that was guarded by a Dwarf. No other treasure in the nine worlds would be great enough to make the recompense that Hreidmar claimed. He thought upon this treasure and he thought on how it might be taken and yet he was ashamed of his thought.

"Dost thou, Loki, know of Andvari's hoard?" he said.

"I know of it," said Loki sharply, "and I know where it is hidden. Wilt thou, Odin, win leave for me to fetch Andvari's hoard?"

Odin spoke to Hreidmar. "I will stay with thee as a hostage," he said, "if thou wilt let this one go to fetch a treasure that will cover the otter's skin hair by hair."

"I will let this be done," said old Hreidmar with the sharp and cunning eyes. "Go now," said he to Loki. Then Loki went from the house.

Andvari was a Dwarf who, in the early days, had gained for himself the greatest treasure in the nine worlds. So that he might guard this treasure unceasingly he changed himself into a fish — into a pike — and he swam in the water before the cave where the hoard was hidden.

All in Asgard knew of the Dwarf and of the hoard he guarded. And there was a thought amongst all that this hoard was not to be meddled with and that some evil was joined to it. But now Odin had given the word that it was to be taken from the Dwarf. Loki set out for Andvari's cave rejoicingly. He came to the pool before the cave and he watched for a sight of Andvari. Soon he saw the pike swimming cautiously before the cave.

He would have to catch the pike and hold him till the treasure was given for ransom. As he watched the pike became aware of him. Suddenly he flung himself forward in the water and went with speed down the stream.

Not with his hands and not with any hook and line could Loki catch that pike. How, then, could he take him? Only with a net that was woven by magic. Then Loki thought of where he might get such a net.

Ran, the wife of old Ægir, the Giant King of the Sea, had a net that was woven by magic. In it she took all that was wrecked on the sea. Loki thought of Ran's net and he turned and went back to Ægir's hall to ask for the Queen. But Ran was seldom in her husband's dwelling. She was now down by the rocks of the sea.

He found Ran, the cold Queen, standing in the flow of the sea, drawing out of the depths with the net that she held in her hands every piece of treasure that was washed that way. She had made a heap of the things she had drawn out of the sea, corals and amber, and bits of gold and silver, but still she was plying her net greedily.

"Thou knowst me, Ægir's wife," said Loki to her.

"I know thee, Loki," said Queen Ran.

"Lend me thy net," said Loki.

"That I will not do," said Queen Ran.

"Lend me thy net that I may catch Andvari the Dwarf who boasts that he has a greater treasure than ever thou wilt take out of the sea," said Loki.

The cold Queen of the sea ceased plying her net. She looked at Loki steadily. Yes, if he were going to catch Andvari she would lend her net to him. She hated all the Dwarfs because this one and that one had told her they had greater treasures than ever she would be mistress of. But especially she hated Andvari, the Dwarf who had the greatest treasure in the nine worlds.

"There is nothing more to gather here," she said, "and if thou wilt swear to bring me back my net by tomorrow I shall lend it to you."

"I swear by the sparks of Muspelheim that I will bring thy net back to thee by tomorrow, O Queen of Ægir," Loki cried. Then Ran put into his hands the Magic Net. Back then he went to where the Dwarf, transformed, was guarding his wondrous hoard.

Dark was the pool in which Andvari floated as a pike; dark it was, but to him it was all golden with the light of his wondrous treasure. For the sake of this hoard he had

given up his companionship with the Dwarfs and his delight in making and shaping the things of their workman-
ship. For the sake of his hoard he had taken on himself
the dumbness and deafness of a fish.

Now as he swam about before the cave he was aware
again of a shadow above him. He slipped toward the
shadow of the bank. Then as he turned round he saw
a net sweeping toward him. He sank down in the water.
But the Magic Net had spread out and he sank into its
meshes.

Suddenly he was out of the water and was left gasping
on the bank. He would have died had he not undone his
transformation.

Soon he appeared as a Dwarf. "Andvari, you are caught;
it is one of the Æsir who has taken you," he heard his
captor say.

"Loki," he gasped.

"Thou art caught and thou shalt be held," Loki said
to him. "It is the will of the Æsir that thou give up thy
hoard to me."

"My hoard, my hoard!" the Dwarf shouted. "Never will
I give up my hoard."

"I hold thee till thou givest it to me," said Loki.

"Unjust, unjust," shouted Andvari. "It is only thou,
Loki, who art unjust. I will go to the throne of Odin and
I will have Odin punish thee for striving to rob me of my
treasure."

"Odin has sent me to fetch thy hoard to him," said Loki.

"Can it be that all the Æsir are unjust? Ah, yes. In the

beginning of things they cheated the Giant who built the wall round their City. The Æsir are unjust."

Loki had Andvari in his power. And after the Dwarf had raged against him and defied him, he tormented him; at last, trembling with rage and with his face covered with tears, Andvari took Loki into his cavern, and, turning a rock aside, showed him the mass of gold and gems that was his hoard.

At once Loki began to gather into the Magic Net lumps and ingots and circlets of gold with gems that were rubies and sapphires and emeralds. He saw Andvari snatch at something on the heap, but he made no sign of marking it. At last all was gathered into the net, and Loki stood there ready to bear the Dwarf's hoard away.

"There is one thing more to be given," said Loki, "the ring that you, Andvari, snatched from the heap."

"I snatched nothing," said the Dwarf. But he shook with anger and his teeth gnashed together and froth came on his lips. "I snatched nothing from the heap."

But Loki pulled up his arm and there fell to the ground the ring that Andvari had hidden under his armpit.

It was the most precious thing in all the hoard. Had it been left with him Andvari would have thought that he still possessed a treasure, for this ring of itself could make gold. It was made out of gold that was refined of all impurities and it was engraven with a rune of power.

Loki took up this most precious ring and put it on his finger. Then the Dwarf screamed at him, turning his thumbs toward him in a curse:

The ring with the rune
Of power upon it:
May it weigh down your fortune,
And load you with evil,
You, Loki, and all
Who lust to possess
The ring I have cherished.

As Andvari uttered this curse Loki saw a figure rise up in the cave and move toward him. As this figure came near he knew who it was: Gulveig, a Giant woman who had once been in Asgard.

Far back in the early days, when the Gods had come to their holy hill and before Asgard was built, three women of the Giants had come amongst the Æsir. After the Three had been with them for a time, the lives of the Æsir changed. Then did they begin to value and to hoard the gold that they had played with. Then did they think of war. Odin hurled his spear amongst the messengers that came from the Vanir, and war came into the world.

The Three were driven out of Asgard. Peace was made with the Vanir. The Apples of Lasting Youth were grown in Asgard. The eagerness for gold was curbed. But never again were the Æsir as happy as they were before the women came to them from the Giants.

Gulveig was one of the Three who had blighted the early happiness of the Gods. And, behold, she was in the cave where Andvari had hoarded his treasure and with a smile upon her face she was advancing toward Loki.

"So, Loki," she said, "thou seest me again. And Odin who sent thee to this cave will see me again. Lo, Loki! I go to Odin to be thy messenger and to tell him that thou comest with Andvari's hoard."

And speaking so, and smiling into his face, Gulveig went out of the cave with swift and light steps. Loki drew the ends of the Magic Net together and gathering all the treasures in its meshes he, too, went out.

Odin, the Eldest of the Gods, stood leaning on his spear and looking at the skin of the otter that was spread out before him. One came into the dwelling swiftly. Odin looked and saw that she who had come in on such swift, glad feet was Gulveig who, once with her two companions, had troubled the happiness of the Gods. Odin raised his spear to cast it at her.

"Lay thy spear down, Odin," she said. "I dwelt for long in the Dwarf's cave. But thy word unloosed me, and the curse said over Andvari's ring has sent me here. Lay thy spear down, and look on me, O Eldest of the Gods.

"Thou didst cast me out of Asgard, but thy word has brought me to come back to thee. And if ye two, Odin and Loki, have bought yourselves free with gold and may enter Asgard, surely I, Gulveig, am free to enter Asgard also."

Odin lowered his spear, sighing deeply. "Surely it is so, Gulveig," he said. "I may not forbid thee to enter Asgard. Would I had thought of giving the man Kvasir's Mead or Mimir's well water rather than this gold as a recompense."

As they spoke Loki came into Hreidmar's dwelling. He laid on the floor the Magic Net. Old Hreidmar with his sharp eyes, and huge Fafnir, and lean and hungry-looking Regin came in to gaze on the gold and gems that shone through the meshes. They began to push each other away from gazing at the gold. Then Hreidmar cried out, "No one may be here but these two kings and I while we measure out the gold and gems and see whether the recompense be sufficient. Go without, go without, sons of mine."

Then Fafnir and Regin were forced to go out of the dwelling. They went out slowly, and Gulveig went with them, whispering to both.

With shaking hands old Hreidmar spread out the skin that once covered his son. He drew out the ears and the tail and the paws so that every single hair could be shown. For long he was on his hands and knees, his sharp eyes searching, searching over every line of the skin. And still on his knees he said, "Begin now, O kings, and cover with a gem or a piece of gold every hair on the skin that was my son's."

Odin stood leaning on his spear, watching the gold and gems being paid out. Loki took the gold — the ingots, and the lumps and the circlets; he took the gems — the rubies, and the emeralds and the sapphires, and he began to place them over each hair. Soon the middle of the skin was all covered. Then he put the gems and the gold over the paws and the tail. Soon the otter-skin was so glittering that one would think it could light up the world. And still Loki went on finding a place where a gem or a piece of gold might be put.

At last he stood up. Every gem and every piece of gold

had been taken out of the net. And every hair on the otter's skin had been covered with a gem or a piece of gold.

And still old Hreidmar on his hands and knees was peering over the skin, searching, searching for a hair that was not covered. At last he lifted himself up on his knees. His mouth was open, but he was speechless. He touched Odin on the knees, and when Odin bent down he showed him a hair upon the lip that was left uncovered.

"What meanest thou?" Loki cried, turning upon the crouching man.

"Your ransom is not paid yet — look, here is still a hair uncovered. You may not go until every hair is covered with gold or a gem."

"Peace, old man," said Loki roughly. "All the Dwarf's hoard has been given thee."

"Ye may not go until every hair has been covered," Hreidmar said again.

"There is no more gold or gems," Loki answered.

"Then ye may not go," cried Hreidmar, springing up.

It was true. Odin and Loki might not leave that dwelling until the recompense they had agreed to was paid in full. Where now would the Æsir go for gold?

And then Odin saw the gleam of gold on Loki's finger: it was the ring he had forced from Andvari. "Thy fingerring," said Odin. "Put thy fingerring over the hair on the otter's skin."

Loki took off the ring that was engraved with the rune of power, and he put it on the lip-hair of the otter's skin. Then Hreidmar clapped his hands and screamed aloud.

Huge Fafnir and lean and hungry-looking Regin came within, and Gulveig came behind them. They stood around the skin of the son and the brother that was all glittering with gold and gems. But they looked at each other more than they looked on the glittering mass, and very deadly were the looks that Fafnir and Regin cast upon their father and cast upon each other.

Over Bifröst, the Rainbow Bridge, went all of the Æsir and the Vanir that had been at old Ægir's feast — Frey and Freya, Frigga, Iduna, and Sif; Tyr with his sword and Thor in his chariot drawn by the goats. Loki came behind them, and behind them all came Odin, the Father of the Gods. He went slowly with his head bent, for he knew that an unwelcome one was following — Gulveig, who once had been cast out of Asgard and whose return now the Gods might not gainsay.

PART III

THE WITCH'S HEART

FOREBODING IN ASGARD

WHAT happened afterwards is to the shame of the Gods, and mortals may hardly speak of it. Gulveig the Witch came into Asgard, for Heimdall might not forbid her entrance. She came within and she had her seat amongst the Æsir and the Vanir. She walked through Asgard with a smile upon her face, and where she walked and where she smiled Care and dire Foreboding came.

Those who felt the care and the foreboding most deeply were Bragi the Poet and his wife, the fair and simple Iduna, she who gathered the apples that kept age from the Dwellers in Asgard. Bragi ceased to tell his never-ending tale. Then one day, overcome by the fear and the foreboding that was creeping through Asgard, Iduna slipped down Ygdrassil, the World Tree, and no one was left to pluck the apples with which the Æsir and the Vanir stayed their youth.

Then were all the Dwellers in Asgard in sore dismay. Strength and beauty began to fade from all. Thor found it hard to lift Miölnir, his great hammer, and the flesh under Freya's necklace lost its white radiance. And still Gulveig the Witch walked smiling through Asgard, although now she was hated by all.

It was Odin and Frey who went in search of Iduna. She would have been found and brought back without delay if Frey had had with him the magic sword that he had bartered for Gerda. In his search he had to strive with one who guarded the lake wherein Iduna had hidden herself. Beli was the one he strove against. He overcame him in the end with a weapon made of stags' antlers. Ah, it was not then but later that Frey lamented the loss of his sword: it was when the Riders of Muspell came against Asgard, and the Vanir, who might have prevailed, prevailed not because of the loss of Frey's sword.

They found Iduna and they brought her back. But still Care and Foreboding crept through Asgard. And it was known, too, that the witch Gulveig was changing the thoughts of the Gods.

At last Odin had to judge Gulveig. He judged her and decreed her death. And only Gungnir, the spear of Odin, might slay Gulveig, who was not of mortal race.

Odin hurled Gungnir. The spear went through Gulveig. But still she stood smiling at the Gods. A second time Odin hurled his spear. A second time Gungnir pierced the witch. She stood livid as one dead but fell not down. A third time Odin hurled his spear. And now, pierced for the third time, the witch gave a scream that made all Asgard shudder and she fell in death on the ground.

"I have slain in these halls where slaying is forbidden," Odin said. "Take now the corpse of Gulveig and burn it on the ramparts, so that no trace of the witch who has troubled us will remain in Asgard."

They brought the corpse of Gulveig the witch out on the ramparts and they lighted fires under the pile on which they laid her and they called upon Hræsvelgur to fan up the flame:

> Hræsvelgur is the Giant,
> Who on heaven's edge sits
> In the guise of an eagle;
> And the winds, it is said,
> Rush down on the earth
> From his outspreading pinions.

Far away was Loki when all this was being done. Often now he went from Asgard, and his journeys were to look upon that wondrous treasure that had passed from the keeping of the Dwarf Andvari. It was Gulveig who had kept the imagination of that treasure within his mind. Now, when he came back and heard the whispers of what had been done, a rage flamed up within him. For Loki was one of those whose minds were being changed by the presence and the whispers of the witch Gulveig. His mind was being changed to hatred of the Gods. Now he went to the place of Gulveig's burning. All her body was in ashes, but her heart had not been devoured by the flames. And Loki in his rage took the heart of the witch and ate it. Oh, black and direful was it in Asgard, the day that Loki ate the heart that the flames would not devour!

LOKI THE BETRAYER

HE stole Frigga's dress of falcon feathers. Then as a falcon he flew out of Asgard. Jötunheim was the place that he flew toward.

The anger and the fierceness of the hawk was within Loki as he flew through the Giants' Realm. The heights and the chasms of that dread land made his spirits mount up like fire. He saw the whirlpools and the smoking mountains and had joy of these sights. Higher and higher he soared until, looking toward the South, he saw the flaming land of Muspelheim. Higher and higher still he soared. With his falcon's eyes he saw the gleam of Surtur's flaming sword. All the fire of Muspelheim and all the gloom of Jötunheim would one day be brought against

Asgard and against Midgard. But Loki was no longer dismayed to think of the ruin of Asgard's beauty and the ruin of Midgard's promise.

He hovered around one of the dwellings in Jötunheim. Why had he come to it? Because he had seen two of the women of that dwelling, and his rage against the Asyniur and the Vanir was such that the ugliness and the evil of these women was pleasing to him.

He hovered before the open door of the Giant's house and he looked upon those who were within. Gerriöd, the most savage of all the Giants, was there. And beside him, squatting on the ground, were his two evil and ugly daughters, Gialp and Greip.

They were big and bulky, black and rugged, with horses' teeth and hair that was like horses' manes. Gialp was the uglier of the two, if one could be said to be uglier than the other, for her nose was a yard long and her eyes were crooked.

What were they talking about as they sat there, one scratching the other? Of Asgard and the Dwellers in Asgard whom they hated. Thor was the one whom they hated most of all, and they were speaking of all they would like to do to him.

"I would keep Thor bound in chains," said Gerriöd the Giant, "and I would beat him to death with my iron club."

"I would grind his bones to powder," said Greip.

"I would tear the flesh off his bones," said Gialp. "Father, can you not catch this Thor and bring him to us alive?"

"Not so long as he has his hammer Miölnir, and the gloves with which he grasps his hammer, and the belt that doubles his strength."

"Oh, if we could catch him without his hammer and his belt and his gloves," cried Gialp and Greip together.

At that moment they saw the falcon hovering before the door. They were eager now for something to hold and torment and so the hearts of the three became set upon catching the falcon. They did not stir from the place where they were sitting, but they called the child Glapp, who was swinging from the roof-tree, and they bade him go out and try to catch the falcon.

All concealed by the great leaves the child Glapp climbed up the ivy that was around the door. The falcon came hovering near. Then Glapp caught it by the wings and fell down through the ivy, screaming and struggling as he was being beaten, and clawed, and torn by the wings and the talons and the beak of the falcon.

Gerriöd and Greip and Gialp rushed out and kept hold of the falcon. As the Giant held him in his hands and looked him over he knew that this was no bird-creature. The eyes showed him to be of Alfheim or Asgard. The Giant took him and shut him in a box till he would speak.

Soon he tapped at the closed box and when Gerriöd opened it Loki spoke to him. So glad was the savage Giant to have one of the Dwellers in Asgard in his power that he and his daughters did nothing but laugh and chuckle to each other for days. And all this time they left Loki in the closed box to waste with hunger.

When they opened the box again Loki spoke to them.

He told them he would do any injury to the Dwellers in Asgard that would please them if they would let him go.

"Will you bring Thor to us?" said Greip.

"Will you bring Thor to us without his hammer, and without the gloves with which he grasps his hammer, and without his belt?" said Gialp.

"I will bring him to you if you will let me go," Loki said. "Thor is easily deceived and I can bring him to you without his hammer and his belt and his gloves."

"We will let you go, Loki," said the Giant, "if you will swear by the gloom of Jötunheim that you will bring Thor to us as you say."

Loki swore that he would do so by the gloom of Jötunheim — "Yea, and by the fires of Muspelheim," he added. The Giant and his daughters let him go, and he flew back to Asgard.

He restored to Frigga her falcon dress. All blamed him for having stolen it, but when he told how he had been shut up without food in Gerriöd's dwelling those who judged him thought he had been punished enough for the theft. He spoke as before to the Dwellers in Asgard, and the rage and hatred he had against them since he had eaten Gulveig's heart he kept from bursting forth.

He talked to Thor of the adventures they had together in Jötunheim. Thor would now roar with laughter when he talked of the time when he went as a bride to Thrym the Giant.

Loki was able to persuade him to make another journey to Jötunheim. "And I want to speak to you of what

I saw in Gerriöd's dwelling," he said. "I saw there the hair of Sif, your wife."

"The hair of Sif, my wife," said Thor in surprise.

"Yes, the hair I once cut off from Sif's head," said Loki. "Gerriöd was the one who found it when I cast it away. They light their hall with Sif's hair. Oh, yes, they don't need torches where Sif's hair is."

"I should like to see it," said Thor.

"Then pay Gerriöd a visit," Loki replied. "But if you go to his house you will have to go without your hammer Miölnir, and without your gloves and your belt."

"Where will I leave Miölnir, and my gloves and my belt?" Thor asked.

"Leave them in Valaskjalf, Odin's own dwelling," said cunning Loki. "Leave them there and come to Gerriöd's dwelling. Surely you will be well treated there."

"Yes, I will leave them in Valaskjalf and go with you to Gerriöd's dwelling," Thor said.

Thor left his hammer, his gloves, and his belt in Valaskjalf. Then he and Loki went toward Jötunheim. When they were near the end of their journey, they came to a wide river, and with a young Giant whom they met on the bank they began to ford it.

Suddenly the river began to rise. Loki and the young Giant would have been swept away only Thor gripped both of them. Higher and higher the river rose, and rougher and rougher it became. Thor had to plant his feet firmly on the bottom or he and the two he held would have been swept down by the flood. He struggled across, holding Loki and the young Giant. A mountain ash grew out of the bank, and, while the two held to him, he grasped it with his hands. The river rose still higher, but Thor was able to draw Loki and the young Giant to the bank, and then he himself scrambled up on it.

Now looking up the river he saw a sight that filled him with rage. A Giantess was pouring a flood into it. This was that was making the river rise and seethe. Thor pulled a rock out of the bank and hurled it at her. It struck her and flung her into the flood. Then she struggled out of the water and went yelping away. This Giantess was Gialp, Gerriöd's ugly and evil daughter.

Nothing would do the young Giant whom Thor had helped across but that the pair would go and visit Grid, his mother, who lived in a cave in the hillside. Loki would not go and was angered to hear that Thor thought of going. But Thor, seeing that the Giant youth was friendly, was willing enough to go to Grid's dwelling.

"Go then, but get soon to Gerriöd's dwelling yonder. I will wait for you there," said Loki. He watched Thor go up the hillside to Grid's cave. He waited until he saw Thor come back down the hillside and go toward Gerriöd's dwelling. He watched Thor go into the house where, as he thought, death awaited him. Then in a madness for what he had done, Loki, with his head drawn down on his shoulders, started running like a bird along the ground.

Grid, the old Giantess, was seated on the floor of the cave grinding corn between two stones. "Who is it?" she said, as her son led Thor within. "One of the Æsir! What Giant do you go to injure now, Asa Thor?"

"I go to injure no Giant, old Grid," Thor replied. "Look upon me! Cannot you see that I have not Miölnir, my mighty hammer, with me, nor my belt, nor my gloves of iron?"

"But where in Jötunheim do you go?"

"To the house of a friendly Giant, old Grid — to the house of Gerriöd."

"Gerriöd a friendly Giant! You are out of your wits, Asa Thor. Is he not out of his wits, my son — this one who saved you from the flood, as you say?"

"Tell him of Gerriöd, old mother," said the Giant youth.

"Do not go to his house, Asa Thor. Do not go to his house."

"My word has been given, and I should be a craven if I stayed away now, just because an old crone sitting at a quernstone tells me I am going into a trap."

"I will give you something that will help you, Asa Thor. Lucky for you I am mistress of magical things. Take this staff in your hands. It is a staff of power and will stand you instead of Miölnir."

"I will take it since you offer it in kindness, old dame, this worm-eaten staff."

"And take these mittens, too. They will serve you for your gauntlets of iron."

"I will take them since you offer them in kindness, old dame, these worn old mittens."

"And take this length of string. It will serve you for your belt of prowess."

"I will take it since you offer it in kindness, old dame, this ragged length of string."

"'Tis well indeed for you, Asa Thor, that I am mistress of magical things."

Thor put the worn length of string around his waist, and as he did he knew that Grid, the old Giantess, was indeed the mistress of magical things. For immediately he felt his strength augmented as when he put on his own belt of strength. He then drew on the mittens and took the staff that she gave him in his hands.

He left the cave of Grid, the old Giantess, and went to Gerriöd's dwelling. Loki was not there. It was then that Thor began to think that perhaps old Grid was right and that a trap was being laid for him.

No one was in the hall. He came out of the hall and into a great stone chamber and he saw no one there either. But in the center of the stone chamber there was a stone seat, and Thor went to it and seated himself upon it.

No sooner was he seated than the chair flew upwards. Thor would have been crushed against the stone roof only that he held his staff up. So great was the power in the staff, so great was the strength that the string around him gave, that the chair was thrust downward. The stone chair crashed down upon the stone floor.

There were horrible screams from under it. Thor lifted up the seat and saw two ugly, broken bodies there. The Giant's daughters, Gialp and Greip, had hidden themselves under the chair to watch his death. But the stone that was to have crushed him against the ceiling had crushed them against the floor.

Thor strode out of that chamber with his teeth set hard. A great fire was blazing in the hall, and standing beside that fire he saw Gerriöd, the long-armed Giant.

He held a tongs into the fire. As Thor came toward him he lifted up the tongs and flung from it a blazing wedge of iron. It whizzed straight toward Thor's forehead. Thor put up his hands and caught the blazing wedge of iron between the mittens that old Grid had given him. Quickly he hurled it back at Gerriöd. It struck the Giant on the forehead and went blazing through him.

Gerriöd crashed down into the fire, and the burning iron made a blaze all around him. And when Thor reached Grid's cave (he went there to restore to the old Giantess the string, the mittens, and the staff of power she had given him) he saw the Giant's dwelling in such a blaze that one would think the fires of Muspelheim. were all around it.

LOKI AGAINST THE AESIR

THE Æsir were the guests of the Vanir: in Frey's palace the Dwellers in Asgard met and feasted in friendship. Odin and Tyr were there, Vidar and Vali, Niörd, Frey, Heimdall, and Bragi. The Asyniur and the Vana were also — Frigga, Freya, Iduna, Gerda, Skadi, Sif, and Nanna. Thor and Loki were not at the feast, for they had left Asgard together.

In Frey's palace the vessels were of shining gold; they made light for the table and they moved of their own accord to serve those who were feasting. All was peace and friendship there until Loki entered the feast hall.

Frey, smiling a welcome, showed a bench to Loki. It was beside Bragi's and next to Freya's. Loki did not take the place; instead he shouted out, "Not beside Bragi will I sit; not beside Bragi, the most craven of all the Dwellers in Asgard."

Bragi sprang up at that affront, but his wife, the mild Iduna, quieted his anger. Freya turned to Loki and reproved him for speaking injurious words at a feast.

"Freya," said Loki, "why were you not so mild when Odur was with you? Would it not have been well to have been wifely with your husband instead of breaking faith with him for the sake of a necklace that you craved of the Giant women?"

Amazement fell on all at the bitterness that was in Loki's words and looks. Tyr and Niörd stood up from their seats. But then the voice of Odin was heard and all was still for the words of the All-Father.

"Take the place beside Vidar, my silent son, O Loki," said Odin, "and let thy tongue which drips bitterness be silent."

"All the Æsir and the Vanir listen to thy words, O Odin, as if thou wert always wise and just," Loki said. "But must we forget that thou didst bring war into the world when thou didst fling thy spear at the envoys of the Vanir? And didst thou not permit me to work craftily on the one who built the wall around Asgard for a price? Thou dost speak, O Odin, and all the Æsir and the Vanir listen to thee! But was it not thou who, thinking not of wisdom but of gold when a ransom had to be made, brought the witch Gulveig out of the cave where she stayed with the Dwarf's treasure? Thou wert not always wise nor always just, O Odin, and we at the table here need not listen to thee as if always thou wert."

Then Skadi, the wife of Niörd, flung words at Loki. She spoke with all the fierceness of her Giant blood. "Why should we not rise up and chase from the hall this chattering crow?" she said.

"Skadi," said Loki, "remember that the ransom for thy father's death has not yet been paid. Thou wert glad to snatch a husband instead of it. Remember who it was that killed thy Giant father. It was I, Loki. And no ransom have I paid thee for it, although thou hast come amongst us in Asgard."

Then Loki fixed his eyes on Frey, the giver of the feast, and all knew that with bitter words he was about to assail him. But Tyr, the brave swordsman, rose up and said, "Not against Frey mayst thou speak, O Loki. Frey is generous; he is the one amongst us who spares the vanquished and frees the captive."

"Cease speaking, Tyr," said Loki. "Thou mayst not always have a hand to hold that sword of thine. Remember this saying of mine in days to come.

"Frey," said he, "because thou art the giver of the feast they think I will not speak the truth about thee. But I am not to be bribed by a feast. Didst thou not send Skirnir to Gymer's dwelling to befool Gymer's flighty daughter? Didst thou not bribe him into frightening her into a marriage with thee, who, men say, wert the slayer of her brother? Yea, Frey. Thou didst part with a charge, with the magic sword that thou shouldst have kept for the battle. Thou hadst cause to grieve when thou didst meet Beli by the lake."

When he said this all who were there of the Vanir rose up, their faces threatening Loki.

"Sit still, ye Vanir," Loki railed. "If the Æsir are to bear the brunt of Jötunheim's and Muspelheim's war upon Asgard it was your part to be the first or the last on Vigard's plain. But already ye have lost the battle for Asgard, for the weapon that was put into Frey's hands he bartered for Gerda the Giantess. Ha! Surtur shall triumph over you because of Frey's bewitchment."

In horror they looked at the one who could let his hatred speak of Surtur's triumph. All would have laid hands on Loki only Odin's voice rang out. Then another appeared at the entrance of the feasting hall. It was Thor. With his hammer upon his shoulder, his gloves of iron on his hands, and his belt of prowess around him, he stood marking Loki with wrathful eyes.

"Ha, Loki, betrayer," he shouted. "Thou didst plan to leave me dead in Gerriöd's house, but now thou wilt meet death by the stroke of this hammer."

His hands were raised to hurl Miölnir. But the words that Odin spoke were heard. "Not in this hall may slaying be done, son Thor. Keep thy hands upon thy hammer."

Then shrinking from the wrath in the eyes of Thor, Loki passed out of the feast hall. He went beyond the walls of Asgard and crossed Bifröst, the Rainbow Bridge. And he cursed Bifröst, and longed to see the day when the armies of Muspelheim would break it down in their rush against Asgard.

East of Midgard there was a place more evil than any region in Jötunheim. It was Jarnvid, the Iron Wood. There dwelt witches who were the most foul of all witches. And they had a queen over them, a hag, mother of many sons who took upon themselves the shapes of wolves. Two of her sons were Skoll and Hati, who pursued Sol, the Sun, and Mani, the Moon. She had a third son, who was Managarm, the wolf who was to be filled with the life-blood of men, who was to swallow up the Moon, and stain the heavens and earth with blood. To Jarnvid, the Iron Wood, Loki made his way. And he wed one of the witches there, Angerboda, and they had children that took on dread shapes. Loki's offspring were the most terrible of the foes that were to come against the Æsir and the Vanir in the time that was called the Twilight of the Gods.

THE VALKYRIE

AGAINST the time when the riders of Muspelheim,
with the Giants and the evil powers of the Under-
world, would bring on battle, Odin All-Father was pre-
paring a host of defenders for Asgard. They were not of
the Æsir nor of the Vanir; they were of the race of mortal
men, heroes chosen from amongst the slain on fields of
battle in Midgard.

To choose the heroes, and to give victory to those
whom he willed to have victory, Odin had battle-maidens
that went to the fields of war. Beautiful were those battle-
maidens and fearless; wise were they also, for to them
Odin showed the Runes of Wisdom. Valkyries, Choosers
of the Slain, they were named.

Those who were chosen on the fields of the slain were called in Asgard the Einherjar. For them Odin made ready a great Hall. Valhalla, the Hall of the Slain, it was called. Five hundred and forty doors had Valhalla, and out of each door eight hundred Champions might pass. Every day the Champions put on their armor and took their weapons down from the walls, and went forth and battled with each other. All who were wounded were made whole again, and in peace and goodly fellowship they sat down to the feast that Odin prepared for them. Odin himself sat with his Champions, drinking wine but eating no meat.

For meat the Champions ate the flesh of the boar Sæhrimnir; every day the boar was killed and cooked, and every morning it was whole again. For drink they had the mead that was made from the milk of the goat Heidrun, the goat that browsed on the leaves of the tree Læradir. And the Valkyries, the wise and fearless battle-maidens, went amongst them, filling up the drinking-horns with the heady mead.

Youngest of all the battle-maidens was Brynhild. Nevertheless, to her Odin All-Father had shown more of the Runes of Wisdom than he had shown to any of her sisters. And when the time came for Brynhild to journey down into Midgard he gave her a swan-feather dress such as he had given before to the three Valkyrie sisters — Alvit, Olrun, and Hladgrun.

In the dazzling plumage of a swan the young battle-maiden flew down from Asgard. Not yet had she to go to the battlefields. Waters drew her, and as she waited on the will of the All-Father she sought out a lake that had golden sands for its shore, and as a maiden bathed in it.

Now there dwelt near this lake a young hero whose name was Agnar. And one day as Agnar lay by the lake he saw a swan with dazzling plumage fly down to it. And while she was in the reeds the swan-feather dress slipped off her, and Agnar beheld the swan change to a maiden.

So bright was her hair, so strong and swift were all her movements, that he knew her for one of Odin's battle-maidens; for one of those who give victory and choose the slain. Very daring was Agnar, and he set his mind upon capturing this battle-maiden even though he should bring on himself the wrath of Odin by doing it.

He hid the swan-feather dress that she had left in the reeds. When she came out of the water she might not fly away. Agnar gave back to her the swan-feather dress, but she had to promise that she would be his battle-maiden.

And as they talked together the young Valkyrie saw in him a hero that one from Asgard might help. Very brave and very noble was Agnar. Brynhild went with him as his battle-maiden, and she told him much from the Runes of Wisdom that she knew, and she showed him that the All-Father's last hope was in the bravery of the heroes of the earth; with the Chosen from the Slain for his Champions he would make battle in defence of Asgard.

Always Brynhild was with Agnar's battalions; above the battles she hovered, her bright hair and flashing battle-dress outshining the spears and swords and shields of the warriors.

But the gray-beard King Helmgunnar made war on

the young Agnar. Odin favored the gray-beard King, and to him he promised the victory. Brynhild knew the will of the All-Father. But to Agnar, not to Helmgunnar, she gave the victory.

Doomed was Brynhild on the instant she went against Odin's will. Never again might she come into Asgard. A mortal woman she was now, and the Norns began to spin the thread of her mortal destiny.

Sorrowful was Odin All-Father that the wisest of his battle-maidens might never appear in Asgard nor walk by the benches at the feasts of his Champions in Valhalla. He rode down on Sleipner to where Brynhild was. And when he came before her it was his, and not her head that was bowed down.

For she knew now that the World of Men was paying a bitter price for the strength that Asgard would have in the last battle. The bravest and noblest were being taken from Midgard to fill up the ranks of Odin's Champions. And Brynhild's heart was full of anger against the rulers of Asgard, and she cared no more to be of them.

Odin looked on his unflinching battle-maiden, and he said, "Is there aught thou wouldst have me bestow on thee in thy mortal life, Brynhild?"

"Naught save this," Brynhild answered, "that in my mortal life no one but a man without fear, the bravest hero in the world, may claim me for wife."

All-Father bowed his head in thought. "It shall be as thou hast asked," he said. "Only he who is without fear shall come near thee."

Then on the top of the mountain that is called Hindfell he had a Hall built that faced the south. Ten Dwarfs built it of black stone. And when the Hall was built he put round it a wall of mounting and circling fire.

More did Odin All-Father: he took a thorn of the Tree of Sleep and he put it into the flesh of the battle-maiden. Then, with her helmet on her head and the breast-mail of the Valkyrie upon her, he lifted Brynhild in his arms and carried her through the wall of mounting and circling fire. He laid her upon the couch that was within the Hall. There she would lie in slumber until the hero who was without fear should ride through the flame and waken her to the life of a mortal woman.

He took farewell of her and he rode back to Asgard on Sleipner. He might not foresee what fate would be hers as a mortal woman. But the fire he had left went mounting and circling around the Hall that the Dwarfs had built. For ages that fire would be a fence around where Brynhild, once a Valkyrie, lay in sleep.

THE CHILDREN OF LOKI

THE children of Loki and the witch Angerboda were not as the children of men: they were formless as water, or air, or fire is formless, but it was given to each of them to take on the form that was most like to their own greed.

Now the Dwellers in Asgard knew that these powers of evil had been born into the world and they thought it well that they should take on forms and appear before them in Asgard. So they sent one to Jarnvid, the Iron Wood, bidding Loki bring before the Gods the powers born of him and the witch Angerboda. So Loki came into Asgard once more. And his offspring took on forms and showed themselves to the Gods. The first, whose greed was destruction, showed himself as a fearful Wolf. Fenrir he was named. And the second, whose greed was slow destruction, showed itself as a Serpent. Jörmungand it was called. The third, whose greed was for withering of all life, took on a form also. When the Gods saw it they were affrighted. For this had the form of a woman, and one side of her was that of a living woman and the other side of her was that of a corpse. Fear ran through Asgard as this form was revealed and as the name that went with it, Hela, was uttered.

Far out of sight of the Gods Hela was thrust. Odin took her and hurled her down to the deeps that are below the world. He cast her down to Niflheim, where she took to herself power over the nine regions. There, in the place that is lowest of all, Hela reigns. Her hall is Elvidnir; it is set round with high walls and it has barred gates; Precipice is the threshold of that hall; Hunger is the table within it; Care is the bed, and Burning Anguish is the hanging of the chamber.

Thor laid hold upon Jörmungand. He flung the serpent into the ocean that engirdles the world. But in the depths of the ocean Jörmungand flourished. It grew and grew until it encircled the whole world. And men knew it as the Midgard Serpent.

Fenrir the Wolf might not be seized upon by any of the Æsir. Fearfully he ranged through Asgard and they were only able to bring him to the outer courts by promising to give him all the food he was able to eat.

The Æsir shrank from feeding Fenrir. But Tyr, the brave swordsman, was willing to bring food to the Wolf's

lair. Every day he brought him huge provision and fed
him with the point of his sword. The Wolf grew and grew
until he became monstrous and a terror in the minds of
the Dwellers in Asgard.

At last the Gods in council considered it and decided
that Fenrir must be bound. The chain that they would
bind him with was called Laeding. In their own smithy
the Gods made it and its weight was greater than Thor's
hammer.

Not by force could the Gods get the fetter upon Fenrir,
so they sent Skirnir, the servant of Frey, to beguile the
Wolf into letting it go upon him. Skirnir came to his lair
and stood near him, and he was dwarfed by the Wolf's
monstrous size.

"How great may thy strength be, Mighty One?" Skirnir
asked. "Couldst thou break this chain easily? The Gods
would try thee."

In scorn Fenrir looked down on the fetter Skirnir
dragged. In scorn he stood still allowing Laeding to be
placed upon him. Then, with an effort that was the least
part of his strength, he stretched himself and broke the
chain in two.

The Gods were dismayed. But they took more iron, and
with greater fires and mightier hammer blows they forged
another fetter. Dromi, this one was called, and it was half
again as strong as Laeding was. Skirnir the Venturesome
brought it to the Wolf's lair, and in scorn Fenrir let the
mightier chain be placed upon him.

He shook himself and the chain held. Then his eyes

became fiery and he stretched himself with a growl and a snarl. Dromi broke across, and Fenrir stood looking balefully at Skirnir.

The Gods saw that no chain they could forge would bind Fenrir and they fell more and more into fear of him. They took council again and they bethought them of the wonder-work the Dwarfs had made for them, the spear Gungnir, the ship Skidbladnir, the hammer Miölnir. Could the Dwarfs be got to make the fetter to bind Fenrir? If they would do it the Gods would add to their domain.

Skirnir went down to Svartheim with the message from Asgard. The Dwarf Chief swelled with pride to think that it was left to them to make the fetter that would bind Fenrir.

"We Dwarfs can make a fetter that will bind the Wolf," he said. "Out of six things we will make it."

"What are these six things?" Skirnir asked.

"The roots of stones, the breath of a fish, the beards of women, the noise made by the footfalls of cats, the sinews of bears, the spittle of a bird."

"I have never heard the noise made by a cat's footfall, nor have I seen the roots of stones nor the beards of women. But use what things you will, O Helper of the Gods."

The Chief brought his six things together and the Dwarfs in their smithy worked for days and nights. They forged a fetter that was named Gleipnir. Smooth and soft as a silken string it was. Skirnir brought it to Asgard and put it into the hands of the Gods.

Then a day came when the Gods said that once again they should try to put a fetter upon Fenrir. But if he was to be bound they would bind him far from Asgard. Lyngvi was an island that they often went to to make sport, and they spoke of going there. Fenrir growled that he would go with them. He came and he sported in his own terrible way. And then as if it were to make more sport, one of the Æsir shook out the smooth cord and showed it to Fenrir.

"It is stronger than you might think, Mighty One," they said. "Will you not let it go upon you that we may see you break it?"

Fenrir out of his fiery eyes looked scorn upon them. "What fame would there be for me," he said, "in breaking such a binding?"

They showed him that none in their company could break it slender as it was. "Thou only art able to break it, Mighty One," they said.

"The cord is slender, but there may be an enchantment in it," Fenrir said.

"Thou canst not break it, Fenrir, and we need not dread thee any more," the Gods said.

Then was the Wolf ravenous wroth, for he lived on the fear that he made in the minds of the Gods. "I am loth to have this binding upon me," he said, "but if one of the Æsir will put his hand in my mouth as a pledge that I shall be freed of it, I will let ye put it on me."

The Gods looked wistfully on one another. It would be health to them all to have Fenrir bound, but who would lose his hand to have it done? One and then another of the

Æsir stepped backward. But not Tyr, the brave swordsman. He stepped to Fenrir and laid his left hand before those tremendous jaws.

"Not thy left hand — thy swordhand, O Tyr," growled Fenrir, and Tyr put his swordhand into that terrible mouth.

Then the cord Gleipnir was put upon Fenrir. With fiery eyes he watched the Gods bind him. When the binding was on him he stretched himself as before. He stretched himself to a monstrous size but the binding did not break off him. Then with fury he snapped his jaws upon the hand, and Tyr's hand, the swordsman's hand, was torn off.

But Fenrir was bound. They fixed a mighty chain to the fetter, and they passed the chain through a hole they bored through a great rock. The monstrous Wolf made terrible efforts to break loose, but the rock and the chain and the fetter held. Then seeing him secured, and to avenge the loss of Tyr's hand, the Gods took Tyr's sword and drove it to the hilt through his underjaw. Horribly the Wolf howled. Mightily the foam flowed down from his jaws. That foam flowing made a river that is called Von — a river of fury that flowed on until Ragnarök came, the Twilight of the Gods.

BALDUR'S DOOM

IN Asgard there were two places that meant strength and joy to the Æsir and the Vanir: one was the garden where grew the apples that Iduna gathered, and the other was the Peace Stead, where, in a palace called Breidablik, Baldur the Well-Beloved dwelt.

In the Peace Stead no crime had ever been committed, no blood had ever been shed, no falseness had ever been spoken. Contentment came into the minds of all in Asgard when they thought upon this place. Ah! Were it not that the Peace Stead was there, happy with Baldur's presence, the minds of the Æsir and the Vanir might have become gloomy and stern from thinking on the direful things that were arrayed against them.

Baldur was beautiful. So beautiful was he that all the white blossoms on the earth were called by his name. Baldur was happy. So happy was he that all the birds on the earth sang his name. So just and so wise was Baldur that the judgment he pronounced might never be altered. Nothing foul or unclean had ever come near where he had his dwelling:

> 'Tis Breidablik called,
> Where Baldur the Fair
> Hath built him a bower,
> In the land where I know
> Least loathliness lies.

Healing things were done in Baldur's Stead. Tyr's wrist was healed of the wounds that Fenrir's fangs had made. And there Frey's mind became less troubled with the foreboding that Loki had filled it with when he railed at him about the bartering of his sword.

Now after Fenrir had been bound to the rock in the faraway island the Æsir and the Vanir knew a while of contentment. They passed bright days in Baldur's Stead, listening to the birds that made music there. And it was there that Bragi the Poet wove into his never-ending story the tale of Thor's adventures amongst the Giants.

But even into Baldur's Stead foreboding came. One day little Hnossa, the child of Freya and the lost Odur, was brought there in such sorrow that no one outside could comfort her. Nanna, Baldur's gentle wife, took the child upon her lap and found ways of soothing her. Then Hnossa told of a dream that had filled her with fright.

She had dreamt of Hela, the Queen that is half living woman and half corpse. In her dream Hela had come into Asgard saying, "A lord of the Æsir I must have to dwell with me in my realm beneath the earth." Hnossa had such fear from this dream that she had fallen into a deep sorrow.

A silence fell upon all when the dream of Hnossa was told. Nanna looked wistfully at Odin All-Father. And Odin, looking at Frigga, saw that a fear had entered her breast.

He left the Peace Stead and went to his watchtower Hlidskjalf. He waited there till Hugin and Munin should come to him. Every day his two ravens flew through the world, and coming back to him told him of all that was happening. And now they might tell him of happenings that would let him guess if Hela had indeed turned her thoughts toward Asgard, or if she had the power to draw one down to her dismal abode.

The ravens flew to him, and lighting one on each of his shoulders, told him of things that were being said up and down Ygdrassil, the World Tree. Ratatösk the Squirrel was saying them. And Ratatösk had heard them from the brood of serpents that with Nidhögg, the great dragon, gnawed ever at the root of Ygdrassil. He told it to the Eagle that sat ever on the topmost bough, that in Hela's habitation a bed was spread and a chair was left empty for some lordly comer.

And hearing this, Odin thought that it were better that Fenrir the Wolf should range ravenously through Asgard

than that Hela should win one from amongst them to fill
that chair and lie in that bed.

He mounted Sleipner, his eight-legged steed, and rode
down toward the abodes of the Dead. For three days and
three nights of silence and darkness he journeyed on. Once
one of the hounds of Helheim broke loose and bayed upon
Sleipner's tracks. For a day and a night Garm, the hound,
pursued them, and Odin smelled the blood that dripped
from his monstrous jaws.

At last he came to where, wrapped in their shrouds, a
field of the Dead lay. He dismounted from Sleipner and
called upon one to rise and speak with him. It was on
Volva, a dead prophetess, he called. And when he pronounced her name he uttered a rune that had the power to
break the sleep of the Dead.

There was a groaning in the middle of where the
shrouded ones lay. Then Odin cried out, "Arise, Volva,
prophetess." There was a stir in the middle of where the
shrouded ones lay, and a head and shoulders were thrust
up from amongst the Dead.

"Who calls on Volva the Prophetess? The rains have
drenched my flesh and the storms have shaken my bones
for more seasons than the living know. No living voice
has a right to call me from my sleep with the Dead."

"It is Vegtam the Wanderer who calls. For whom is the
bed prepared and the seat left empty in Hela's habitation?"

"For Baldur, Odin's son, is the bed prepared and the
seat left empty. Now let me go back to my sleep with the
Dead."

But now Odin saw beyond Volva's prophecy. "Who is

it," he cried out, "that stands with unbowed head and that will not lament for Baldur? Answer, Volva, prophetess!"

"Thou seest far, but thou canst not see clearly. Thou art Odin. I can see clearly but I cannot see far. Now let me go back to my sleep with the Dead."

"Volva, prophetess!" Odin cried out again.

But the voice from amongst the shrouded ones said, "Thou canst not wake me any more until the fires of Muspelheim blaze above my head."

Then there was silence in the field of the Dead, and Odin turned Sleipner, his steed, and for four days, through the gloom and silence, he journeyed back to Asgard.

Frigga had felt the fear that Odin had felt. She looked toward Baldur, and the shade of Hela came between her and her son. But then she heard the birds sing in the Peace Stead and she knew that none of all the things in the world would injure Baldur.

And to make it sure she went to all the things that could hurt him and from each of them she took an oath that it would not injure Baldur, the Well-Beloved. She took an oath from fire and from water, from iron and from all metals, from earths and stones and great trees, from birds and beasts and creeping things, from poisons and diseases. Very readily they all gave the oath that they would work no injury on Baldur.

Then when Frigga went back and told what she had accomplished the gloom that had lain on Asgard lifted. Baldur would be spared to them. Hela might have a place prepared in her dark habitation, but neither fire nor water, nor iron nor any metals, nor earths nor stones nor great woods, nor birds nor beasts nor creeping things, nor poisons nor diseases, would help her to bring him down. "Hela has no arms to draw you to her," the Æsir and the Vanir cried to Baldur.

Hope was renewed for them and they made games to honor Baldur. They had him stand in the Peace Stead and they brought against him all the things that had sworn to leave him hurtless. And neither the battle-axe flung full at him, nor the stone out of the sling, nor the burning brand, nor the deluge of water would injure the beloved of Asgard. The Æsir and the Vanir laughed joyously to see these things fall harmlessly from him while a throng came to join them in the games; Dwarfs and friendly Giants.

But Loki the Hater came in with that throng. He watched the games from afar. He saw the missiles and the weapons being flung and he saw Baldur stand smiling and happy under the strokes of metal and stones and great woods. He wondered at the sight, but he knew that he might not ask the meaning of it from the ones who knew him.

He changed his shape into that of an old woman and he went amongst those who were making sport for Baldur. He spoke to Dwarfs and friendly Giants. "Go to Frigga and ask. Go to Frigga and ask," was all the answer Loki got from any of them.

Then to Fensalir, Frigga's mansion, Loki went. He told those in the mansion that he was Groa, the old Enchantress who was drawing out of Thor's head the fragments of a grindstone that a Giant's throw had embedded in it. Frigga knew about Groa and she praised the Enchantress for what she had done.

"Many fragments of the great grindstone have I taken out of Thor's head by the charms I know," said the pretended Groa. "Thor was so grateful that he brought back to me the husband that he once had carried off to the end of the earth. So overjoyed was I to find my husband restored that I forgot the rest of the charms. And I left some fragments of the stone in Thor's head."

So Loki said, repeating a story that was true. "Now I remember the rest of the charm," he said, "and I can draw out the fragments of the stone that are left. But will you not tell me, O Queen, what is the meaning of the extraordinary things I saw the Æsir and the Vanir doing?"

"I will tell you," said Frigga, looking kindly and happily at the pretended old woman. "They are hurling all manner of heavy and dangerous things at Baldur, my beloved son. And all Asgard cheers to see that neither metal nor stone nor great wood will hurt him."

"But why will they not hurt him?" said the pretended Enchantress.

"Because I have drawn an oath from all dangerous and threatening things to leave Baldur hurtless," said Frigga.

"From all things, lady? Is there no thing in all the world that has not taken an oath to leave Baldur hurtless?"

"Well, indeed, there is one thing that has not taken the oath. But that thing is so small and weak that I passed it by without taking thought of it."

"What can it be, lady?"

"The Mistletoe that is without root or strength. It grows on the eastern side of Valhalla. I passed it by without drawing an oath from it."

"Surely you were not wrong to pass it by. What could the Mistletoe — the rootless Mistletoe — do against Baldur?"

Saying this the pretended Enchantress hobbled off.

But not far did the pretender go hobbling. He changed his gait and hurried to the eastern side of Valhalla. There a great oak tree flourished and out of a branch of it a little bush of Mistletoe grew. Loki broke off a spray and with it in his hand he went to where the Æsir and the Vanir were still playing games to honor Baldur.

All were laughing as Loki drew near, for the Giants and the Dwarfs, the Asyniur and the Vana, were all casting missiles. The Giants threw too far and the Dwarfs could not throw far enough, while the Asyniur and the Vana threw far and wide of the mark. In the midst of all that glee and gamesomeness it was strange to see one standing joyless. But one stood so, and he was of the Æsir — Hödur, Baldur's blind brother.

"Why do you not enter the game?" said Loki to him in his changed voice.

"I have no missile to throw at Baldur," Hödur said.

"Take this and throw it," said Loki. "It is a twig of the Mistletoe."

"I cannot see to throw it," said Hödur.

"I will guide your hand," said Loki. He put the twig of Mistletoe in Hödur's hand and he guided the hand for the throw. The twig flew toward Baldur. It struck him on the breast and it pierced him. Then Baldur fell down with a deep groan.

The Æsir and the Vanir, the Dwarfs and the friendly Giants, stood still in doubt and fear and amazement. Loki slipped away. And blind Hödur, from whose hand the twig of Mistletoe had gone, stood quiet, not knowing that his throw had bereft Baldur of life.

Then a wailing rose around the Peace Stead. It was from the Asyniur and the Vana. Baldur was dead, and they began to lament him. And while they were lamenting him, the beloved of Asgard, Odin came amongst them.

"Hela has won our Baldur from us," Odin said to Frigga as they both bent over the body of their beloved son.

"Nay, I will not say it," Frigga said.

When the Æsir and the Vanir had won their senses back the mother of Baldur went amongst them. "Who amongst you would win my love and goodwill?" she said. "Whoever would let him ride down to Hela's dark realm and ask the Queen to take ransom for Baldur. It may be she will take it and let Baldur come back to us. Who amongst you will go? Odin's steed is ready for the journey."

Then forth stepped Hermod the Nimble, the brother of Baldur. He mounted Sleipner and turned the eight-legged steed down toward Hela's dark realm.

For nine days and nine nights Hermod rode on. His way was through rugged glens, one deeper and darker than the other. He came to the river that is called Giöll and to the bridge across it that is all glittering with gold. The pale maid who guards the bridge spoke to him.

"The hue of life is still on thee," said Modgudur, the pale maid. "Why dost thou journey down to Hela's deathly realm?"

"I am Hermod," he said, "and I go to see if Hela will take ransom for Baldur."

"Fearful is Hela's habitation for one to come to," said Modgudur, the pale maid. "All round it is a steep wall that even thy steed might hardly leap. Its threshold is Precipice. The bed therein is Care, the table is Hunger, the hanging of the chamber is Burning Anguish."

"It may be that Hela will take ransom for Baldur."

"If all things in the world still lament for Baldur, Hela will have to take ransom and let him go from her," said Modgudur, the pale maid that guards the glittering bridge.

"It is well, then, for all things lament Baldur. I will go to her and make her take ransom."

"Thou mayst not pass until it is of a surety that all things still lament him. Go back to the world and make sure. If thou dost come to this glittering bridge and tell me that all things still lament Baldur, I will let thee pass and Hela will have to hearken to thee."

"I will come back to thee, and thou, Modgudur, pale maid, wilt have to let me pass."

"Then I will let thee pass," said Modgudur.

Joyously Hermod turned Sleipner and rode back through the rugged glens, each one less gloomy than the other. He reached the upper world, and saw that all things were still lamenting for Baldur. Joyously Hermod rode onward. He met the Vanir in the middle of the world and he told them the happy tidings.

Then Hermod and the Vanir went through the world seeking out each thing and finding that each thing still wept for Baldur. But one day Hermod came upon a crow that was sitting on the dead branch of a tree. The crow made no lament as he came near. She rose up and flew away and Hermod followed her to make sure that she lamented for Baldur.

He lost sight of her near a cave. And then before the cave he saw a hag with blackened teeth who raised no voice of lament. "If thou art the crow that came flying here, make lament for Baldur," Hermod said.

"I, Thaukt, will make no lament for Baldur," the hag said, "let Hela keep what she holds."

"All things weep tears for Baldur," Hermod said.

"I will weep dry tears for him," said the hag.

She hobbled into her cave, and as Hermod followed a crow fluttered out. He knew that this was Thaukt, the evil hag, transformed. He followed her, and she went through the world croaking, "Let Hela keep what she holds. Let Hela keep what she holds."

Then Hermod knew that he might not ride to Hela's habitation. All things knew that there was one thing in the world that would not lament for Baldur. The Vanir came back to him, and with head bowed over Sleipner's mane, Hermod rode into Asgard.

Now the Æsir and the Vanir, knowing that no ransom would be taken for Baldur and that the joy and content of Asgard were gone indeed, made ready his body for the burning. First they covered Baldur's body with a rich robe, and each left beside it his most precious possession. Then they all took leave of him, kissing him upon the brow. But Nanna, his gentle wife, flung herself on his dead breast and her heart broke and she died of her grief. Then did the Æsir and the Vanir weep afresh. And they took the body of Nanna and they placed it side by side with Baldur's.

On his own great ship, Ringhorn, would Baldur be placed with Nanna beside him. Then the ship would be launched on the water and all would be burned with fire.

But it was found that none of the Æsir or the Vanir were able to launch Baldur's great ship. Hyrroken, a Giantess, was sent for. She came mounted on a great wolf with twisted serpents for a bridle. Four Giants held fast the wolf when she alighted. She came to the ship and with a single push she sent it into the sea. The rollers struck out fire as the ship dashed across them.

Then when it rode the water fires mounted on the ship. And in the blaze of the fires one was seen bending over the body of Baldur and whispering into his ear. It was Odin All-Father. Then he went down off the ship and all the fires rose into a mighty burning. Speechlessly the Æsir and the Vanir watched with tears streaming down their faces while all things lamented, crying, "Baldur the Beautiful is dead, is dead."

And what was it that Odin All-Father whispered to Baldur as he bent above him with the flames of the burning ship around? He whispered of a heaven above Asgard that Surtur's flames might not reach, and of a life that would come to beauty again after the World of Men and the World of the Gods had been searched through and through with fire.

LOKI'S PUNISHMENT

THE crow went flying toward the North, croaking as she flew, "Let Hela keep what she holds. Let Hela keep what she holds." That crow was the hag Thaukt transformed, and the hag Thaukt was Loki.

He flew to the North and came into the wastes of Jötunheim. As a crow he lived there, hiding himself from the wrath of the Gods. He told the Giants that the time had come for them to build the ship Naglfar, the ship that was to be built out of the nails of dead men, and that was to sail to Asgard on the day of Ragnarök with the Giant Hrymer steering it. And harkening to what he said the Giants then and there began to build Naglfar, the ship that Gods and men wished to remain unbuilt for long.

Then Loki, tiring of the wastes of Jötunheim, flew to the burning South. As a lizard he lived amongst the rocks of Muspelheim, and he made the Fire Giants rejoice when he told them of the loss of Frey's sword and of Tyr's right hand.

But still in Asgard there was one who wept for Loki — Siguna, his wife. Although he had left her and had shown his hatred for her, Siguna wept for her evil husband.

He left Muspelheim as he had left Jötunheim and he came to live in the World of Men. He knew that he had now come into a place where the wrath of the Gods might find him, and so he made plans to be ever ready for escape. He had come to the River where, ages before, he had slain the otter that was the son of the Enchanter, and on the very rock where the otter had eaten the salmon on the day of his killing, Loki built his house. He made four doors to it so that he might see in every direction. And the power that he kept for himself was the power of transforming himself into a salmon.

Often as a salmon he swam in the River. But even for the fishes that swam beside him Loki had hatred. Out of flax and yarn he wove a net that men might have the means of taking them out of the water.

The wrath that the Gods had against Loki did not pass away. It was he who, as Thaukt, the Hag, had given Hela the power to keep Baldur unransomed. It was he who had put into Hödur's hand the sprig of Mistletoe that had bereft Baldur of life. Empty was Asgard now that Baldur lived no more in the Peace Stead, and stern and gloomy grew the minds of the Æsir and the Vanir with thinking on the direful things that were arrayed against them. Odin in his hall of Valhalla thought only of the ways by which he could bring heroes to him to be his help in defending Asgard.

The Gods searched through the world and they found at last the place where Loki had made his dwelling. He was weaving the net to take fishes when he saw them coming from four directions. He threw the net into the fire so that it was burnt, and he sprang into the River and transformed himself into a salmon. When the Gods entered his dwelling they found only the burnt-out fire.

But there was one amongst them who could understand all that he saw. In the ashes were the marks of the burnt net and he knew that these were the tracing of something to catch fishes. And from the marks left in the ashes he made a net that was the same as the one Loki had burnt.

With it in their hands the Gods went down the River, dragging the net through the water. Loki was affrighted to find the thing of his own weaving brought against him. He lay between two stones at the bottom of the River, and the net passed over him.

But the Gods knew that the net had touched something at the bottom. They fastened weights to it and they dragged the net through the River again. Loki knew that he might not escape it this time and he rose in the water and swam toward the sea. The Gods caught sight of him as he leaped over a waterfall. They followed him, dragging the net. Thor waded behind, ready to seize him should he turn back.

Loki came out at the mouth of the River and behold! There was a great eagle hovering over the waves of the sea and ready to swoop down on fishes. He turned back in the

River. He made a leap that took him over the net that the Gods were dragging. But Thor was behind the net and he caught the salmon in his powerful hands and he held him for all the struggle that Loki made. No fish had ever struggled so before. Loki got himself free all but his tail, but Thor held to the tail and brought him amongst the rocks and forced him to take on his proper form.

He was in the hands of those whose wrath was strong against him. They brought him to a cavern and they bound him to three sharp-pointed rocks. With cords that were made of the sinews of wolves they bound him, and they transformed the cords into iron bands. There they would have left Loki bound and helpless. But Skadi, with her fierce Giant blood, was not content that he should be left untormented. She found a serpent that had deadly venom and she hung this serpent above Loki's head. The drops of venom fell upon him, bringing him anguish drop by drop, minute by minute. So Loki's torture went on.

But Siguna with the pitying heart came to his relief. She exiled herself from Asgard, and endured the darkness and the cold of the cavern, that she might take some of the torment away from him who was her husband. Over Loki Siguna stood, holding in her hands a cup into which fell the serpent's venom, thus sparing him from the full measure of anguish. Now and then Siguna had to turn aside to spill out the flowing cup, and then the drops of venom fell upon Loki and he screamed in agony, twisting in his bonds. It was then that men felt the earth quake. There in his bonds Loki stayed until the coming of Ragnarök, the Twilight of the Gods.

PART IV

THE SWORD OF THE
VOLSUNGS AND THE
TWILIGHT OF THE GODS

SIGURD'S YOUTH

IN Midgard, in a northern Kingdom, a King reigned whose name was Alv; he was wise and good, and he had in his house a fosterson whose name was Sigurd.

Sigurd was fearless and strong; so fearless and so strong was he that he once captured a bear of the forest and drove him to the King's Hall. His mother's name was Hiordis. Once, before Sigurd was born, Alv and his father who was King before him went on an expedition across the sea and came into another country. While they were yet afar off they heard the din of a great battle. They came to the battlefield, but they found no living warriors on it, only heaps of slain. One warrior they marked: he was white-bearded and old and yet he seemed the noblest-looking man Alv or his father had ever looked on. His arms showed that he was a King amongst one of the bands of warriors.

They went through the forest searching for survivors of the battle. And, hidden in a dell in the forest, they came upon two women. One was tall with blue, unflinching eyes and ruddy hair, but wearing the garb of a serving-maid. The other wore the rich dress of a Queen, but she was of low stature and her manner was covert and shrinking.

When Alv and his father drew near, the one who had on her the raiment of a Queen said, "Help us, lords, and protect us, and we will show you where a treasure is hidden. A great battle has been fought between the men of King Lygni and the men of King Sigmund, and the men of King Lygni have won the victory and have gone from the field. But King Sigmund is slain, and we who are of his household hid his treasure and we can show it to you."

"The noble warrior, white-haired and white-bearded, who lies yonder — is he King Sigmund?"

The woman answered, "Yes, lord, and I am his Queen."

"We have heard of King Sigmund," said Alv's father. "His fame and the fame of his race, the Volsungs, is over the wide world."

Alv said no word to either of the women, but his eyes stayed on the one who had on the garb of a serving-maid. She was on her knees, wrapping in a beast's skin two pieces of a broken sword.

"You will surely protect us, good lords," said she who had on the queenly dress.

"Yea, wife of King Sigmund, we will protect you and your serving-maid," said Alv's father, the old King.

Then the women took the warriors to a wild place on the seashore and they showed them where King Sigmund's treasure was hidden amongst the rocks: cups of gold and mighty armrings and jeweled collars. Prince Alv and his father put the treasure on the ship and brought the two women aboard. Then they sailed from the land.

That was before Sigurd, the fosterson of King Alv, was born.

Now the mother of Alv was wise and little of what she saw escaped her noting. She saw that of the two women that her son and her husband had brought into their kingdom, the one who wore the dress of the serving-maid had unflinching eyes and a high beauty, while the one who wore the queenly dress was shrinking and unstately. One night when all the women of the household were sitting round her, spinning wool by the light of torches in the hall, the Queen-mother said to the one who wore the queenly garb:

"Thou art good at rising in the morning. How dost thou know in the dark hours when it wears to dawn?"

The one clad in the queenly garb said, "When I was young I used to rise to milk the cows, and I waken ever since at the same hour."

The Queen-mother said to herself, "It is a strange country in which the royal maids rise to milk the cows."

Then she said to the one who wore the clothes of the serving-maid:

"How dost thou know in the dark hours when the dawn is coming?"

"My father," she said, "gave me the ring of gold that I wear, and always before it is time to rise I feel it grow cold on my finger."

"It is a strange country, truly," said the Queen-mother to herself, "in which the serving-maids wear rings of gold."

When all the others had left she spoke to the two women who had been brought into her country. To the one who wore the clothes of a serving-maid she said:

"Thou art the Queen."

Then the one who wore the queenly clothes said, "Thou art right, lady. She is the Queen, and I cannot any longer pretend to be other than I am."

Then the other woman spoke. Said she: "I am the Queen as thou hast said — the Queen of King Sigmund who was slain. Because a King sought for me I changed clothes with my serving-maid, my wish being to baffle those who might be sent to carry me away.

"Know that I am Hiordis, a King's daughter. Many men came to my father to ask for me in marriage, and of those that came there were two whom I heard much of: one was King Lygni and the other was King Sigmund of the race of the Volsungs. The King, my father, told me it was for me to choose between these two. Now King Sigmund was old, but he was the most famous warrior in the whole world, and I chose him rather than King Lygni.

"We were wed. But King Lygni did not lose desire of me, and in a while he came against King Sigmund's kingdom with a great army of men. We hid our treasure by the seashore, and I and my maid watched the battle from the borders of the forest. With the help of Gram, his wondrous sword, and his own great warrior strength, Sigmund was able to harry the great force that came against him. But suddenly he was stricken down. Then was the battle lost. Only King Lygni's men survived it, and they scattered to search for me and the treasure of the King.

"I came to where my lord lay on the field of battle, and he raised himself on his shield when I came, and he told me that death was very near him. A stranger had entered the battle at the time when it seemed that the men of King Lygni must draw away. With the spear that he held in his hand he struck at Sigmund's sword, and Gram, the wondrous sword, was broken in two pieces. Then did King Sigmund get his death-wound. 'It must be I shall die,' he said, 'for the spear against which my sword broke was Gungnir, Odin's spear. Only that spear could have shattered the sword that Odin gave my fathers. Now must I go to Valhalla, Odin's Hall of Heroes.'

" 'I weep,' I said, 'because I have no son who might call himself of the great race of the Volsungs.'

" 'For that you need not weep,' said Sigmund, 'a son will be born to you, my son and yours, and you shall name him Sigurd. Take now the broken pieces of my wondrous sword and give them to my son when he shall be of warrior age.'

"Then did Sigmund turn his face to the ground and the death-struggle came on him. Odin's Valkyrie took his spirit from the battlefield. And I lifted up the broken pieces of the sword, and with my serving-maid I went and hid in a deep dell in the forest. Then your husband and your son found us and they brought us to your kingdom where we have been kindly treated, O Queen."

Such was the history that Hiordis, the wife of King Sigmund, told to the mother of Prince Alv.

Soon afterwards the child was born to her that was Sigmund's son. Sigurd she named him. And after Sigurd was born the old King died and Prince Alv became King in his stead. He married Hiordis, she of the ruddy hair, the unflinching ways, and the high beauty, and he brought up her son Sigurd in his house as his fosterson.

Sigurd, the son of Sigmund, before he came to warrior's age, was known for his strength and his swiftness and for the fearlessness that shone round him like a glow. "Mighty was the race he sprang from, the Volsung race," men said, "but Sigurd will be as mighty as any that have gone before him." He built himself a hut in the forest that he might hunt wild beasts and live near to one who was to train him in many crafts.

This one was Regin, a maker of swords and a cunning man besides. It was said of Regin that he was an Enchanter and that he had been in the world for longer than the generations of men. No one remembered, nor no one's father remembered, when Regin had come into that country. He taught Sigurd the art of working in metals and he taught him, too, the lore of other days. But ever as he taught him he looked at Sigurd strangely, not as a man looks at his fellow, but as a lynx looks at a stronger beast.

One day Regin said to young Sigurd, "King Alv has thy father's treasure, men say, and yet he treats thee as if thou wert thrall-born."

Now Sigurd knew that Regin said this that he might anger him and thereafter use him to his own ends. He said, "King Alv is a wise and a good King, and he would let me have riches if I had need of them."

"Thou dost go about as a footboy, and not as a King's son."

"Any day that it likes me I might have a horse to ride," Sigurd said.

"So thou dost say," said Regin, and he turned from Sigurd and went to blow the fire of his smithy.

Sigurd was made angry and he threw down the irons on which he was working and he ran to the horse-pastures by the great River. A herd of horses was there, gray and black and roan and chestnut, the best of the horses that King Alv possessed. As he came near to where the herd grazed he saw a stranger near, an ancient but robust man, wearing a strange cloak of blue and leaning on a staff to watch the horses. Sigurd, though young, had seen Kings in their halls, but this man had a bearing that was more lofty than any King's he had ever looked on.

"Thou art going to choose a horse for thyself," said the stranger to Sigurd.

"Yea, father," Sigurd said.

"Drive the herd first into the River," the stranger said.

Sigurd drove the horses into the wide River. Some were swept down by the current, others struggled back and clambered up the bank of the pastures. But one swam across the river, and throwing up his head neighed as for a victory. Sigurd marked him; a gray horse he was, young and proud, with a great flowing mane. He went through the water and caught this horse, mounted him, and brought him back across the River.

"Thou hast done well," said the stranger. "Grani, whom thou hast got, is of the breed of Sleipner, the horse of Odin."

"And I am of the race of the sons of Odin," cried Sigurd, his eyes wide and shining with the very light of the sun. "I am of the race of the sons of Odin, for my father was Sigmund, and his father was Volsung, and his father was Rerir, and his father was Sigi, who was the son of Odin."

The stranger, leaning on his staff looked on the youth steadily. Only one of his eyes was to be seen, but that eye, Sigurd thought, might see through a stone. "All thou hast named," the stranger said, "were as swords of Odin to send men to Valhalla, Odin's Hall of Heroes. And of all that thou hast named there were none but were chosen by Odin's Valkyries for battles in Asgard."

Cried Sigurd, "Too much of what is brave and noble in the world is taken by Odin for his battles in Asgard."

The stranger leaned on his staff and his head was bowed. "What wouldst thou?" he said, and it did not seem to Sigurd that he spoke to him. "What wouldst thou? The

leaves wither and fall off Ygdrassil, and the day of Ragnarök comes." Then he raised his head and spoke to
Sigurd. "The time is near," he said, "when thou mayst
possess thyself of the pieces of thy father's sword."

Then the man in the strange cloak of blue went climb-
ing up the hill and Sigurd watched him pass away from his
sight. He had held back Grani, his proud horse, but now
he turned him and let him gallop along the River in a race
that was as swift as the wind.

THE SWORD GRAM AND
THE DRAGON FAFNIR

MOUNTED upon Grani, his proud horse, Sigurd rode
to the Hall and showed himself to Alv, the King,
and to Hiordis, his mother. Before the Hall he shouted
out the Volsung name, and King Alv felt as he watched
him that this youth was a match for a score of men, and
Hiordis, his mother, saw the blue flame of his eyes and
thought to herself that his way through the world would
be as the way of the eagle through the air.

Having shown himself before the Hall, Sigurd dismounted from Grani, and stroked and caressed him with
his hands and told him that now he might go back and

take pasture with the herd. The proud horse breathed fondly over Sigurd and bounded away.

Then Sigurd strode on until he came to the hut in the forest where he worked with the cunning smith Regin. No one was in the hut when he entered. But over the anvil, in the smoke of the smithy fire, there was a work of Regin's hands. Sigurd looked upon it, and a hatred for the thing that was shown rose up in him.

The work of Regin's hands was a shield, a great shield of iron. Hammered out on that shield and colored with red and brown colors was the image of a Dragon, a Dragon lengthening himself out of a cave. Sigurd thought it was the image of the most hateful thing in the world, and the light of the smithy fire falling on it, and the smoke of the smithy fire rising round it, made it seem verily a Dragon living in his own element of fire and reek.

While he was still gazing on the loathly image, Regin, the cunning smith, came into the smithy. He stood by the wall and he watched Sigurd. His back was bent; his hair fell over his eyes that were all fiery, and he looked like a beast that runs behind the hedges.

"Aye, thou dost look on Fafnir the Dragon, son of the Volsungs," he said to Sigurd. "Mayhap it is thou who wilt slay him."

"I would not strive with such a beast. He is all horrible to me," Sigurd said.

"With a good sword thou mightst slay him and win for thyself more renown than ever thy fathers had," Regin whispered.

"I shall win renown as my fathers won renown, in battle with men and in conquest of kingdoms," Sigurd said.

"Thou art not a true Volsung or thou wouldst gladly go where most danger and dread is," said Regin. "Thou hast heard of Fafnir the Dragon, whose image I have wrought here. If thou dost ride to the crest of the hills thou mayst look across to the desolate land where Fafnir has his haunt. Know that once it was fair land where men had peace and prosperity, but Fafnir came and made his den in a cave near by, and his breathings as he went to and came from the River withered up the land and made it the barren waste that men called Gnita Heath. Now, if thou art a true Volsung, thou wilt slay the Dragon, and let that land become fair again, and bring the people back to it and so add to King Alv's domain."

"I have nought to do with the slaying of Dragons," Sigurd said. "I have to make war on King Lygni, and avenge upon him the slaying of Sigmund, my father."

"What is the slaying of Lygni and the conquest of his kingdom to the slaying of Fafnir the Dragon?" Regin cried. "I will tell thee what no one else knows of Fafnir the Dragon. He guards a hoard of gold and jewels the like of which was never seen in the world. All this hoard you can make yours by slaying him."

"I do not covet riches," Sigurd said.

"No riches is like to the riches that Fafnir guards. His hoard is the hoard that the Dwarf Andvari had from the world's early days. Once the Gods themselves paid it over as a ransom. And if thou wilt win this hoard thou wilt be as one of the Gods."

"How dost thou know that of which thou speakst, Regin?" Sigurd said.

"I know, and one day I may tell thee how I know."

"And one day I may harken to thee. But speak to me no more of this Dragon. I would have thee make a sword, a sword that will be mightier and better shapen than any sword in the world. Thou canst do this, Regin, for thou art accounted the best swordsmith amongst men."

Regin looked at Sigurd out of his small and cunning eyes and he thought it was best to make himself active. So he took the weightiest pieces of iron and put them into his furnace and he brought out the secret tools that he used when a masterwork was claimed from his hands.

All day Sigurd worked beside him keeping the fire at its best glow and bringing water to cool the blade as it was fashioned and refashioned. And as he worked he thought only about the blade and about how he would make war upon King Lygni, and avenge the man who was slain before he himself was born.

All day he thought only of war and of the beaten blade. But at night his dreams were not upon wars nor shapen blades but upon Fafnir the Dragon. He saw the heath that was left barren by his breath, and he saw the cave where he had his den, and he saw him crawling down from his cave, his scales glittering like rings of mail, and his length the length of a company of men on the march.

The next day he worked with Regin to shape the great sword. When it was shapen with all the cunning Regin knew it looked indeed a mighty sword. Then Regin sharpened it and Sigurd polished it. And at last he held the great sword by its iron hilt.

Then Sigurd took the shield that had the image of Fafnir the Dragon upon it and he put the shield over the anvil of the smithy. Raising the great sword in both his hands he struck full on the iron shield.

The stroke of the sword sheared away some of the shield, but the blade broke in Sigurd's hands. Then in anger he turned on Regin, crying out, "Thou hast made a knave's sword for me. To work with thee again! Thou must make me a Volsung's sword."

Then he went out and called to Grani, his horse, and mounted him and rode to the river bank like the sweep of the wind.

Regin took more pieces of iron and began to forge a new sword, uttering as he worked runes that were about the hoard that Fafnir the Dragon guarded. And Sigurd that night dreamt of glittering treasure that he coveted not, masses of gold and heaps of glistening jewels.

He was Regin's help the next day and they both worked to make a sword that would be mightier than the first. For three days they worked upon it, and then Regin put into Sigurd's hands a sword, sharpened and polished, that was mightier and more splendid looking than the one that had been forged before. And again Sigurd took the shield that had the image of the Dragon upon it and he put it upon the anvil. Then he raised his arms and struck his full blow. The sword cut through the shield, but when it struck the anvil it shivered in his hands.

He left the smithy angrily and called to Grani, his proud horse. He mounted and rode on like the sweep of the wind.

Later he came to his mother's bower and stood before Hiordis. "A greater sword must I have," said he, "than one that is made of metal dug out of the earth. The time has come, mother, when thou must put into my hands the broken pieces of Gram, the sword of Sigmund and the Volsungs."

Hiordis measured him with the glance of her eyes, and she saw that her son was a mighty youth and one fit to use the sword of Sigmund and the Volsungs. She bade him go with her to the King's Hall. Out of the great stone chest that was in her chamber she took the beast's skin and the broken blade that was wrapped in it. She gave the pieces into the hands of her son. "Behold the halves of Gram," she said, "of Gram, the mighty sword that in the far-off days Odin left in the Branstock, in the tree of the house of Volsung. I would see Gram new-shapen in thy hands, my son."

Then she embraced him as she had never embraced him before, and standing there with her ruddy hair about her she told him of the glory of Gram and of the deeds of his fathers in whose hands the sword had shone.

Then Sigurd went to the smithy, and he wakened Regin out of his sleep, and he made him look on the shining halves of Sigmund's sword. He commanded him to make out of these halves a sword for his hand.

Regin worked for days in his smithy and Sigurd never left his side. At last the blade was forged, and when Sigurd held it in his hand fire ran along the edge of it.

Again he laid the shield that had the image of the Dragon upon it on the anvil of the smithy. Again, with his hands on its iron hilt, he raised the sword for a full stroke. He struck, and the sword cut through the shield and sheared through the anvil, cutting away its iron horn. Then did Sigurd know that he had in his hands the Volsungs' sword. He went without and called to Grani, and like the sweep of the wind rode down to the River's bank. Shreds of wool were floating down the water. Sigurd struck at them with his sword, and the fine wool was divided against the water's edge. Hardness and fineness, Gram could cut through both.

That night Gram, the Volsungs' sword, was under his head when he slept, but still his dreams were filled with images that he had not regarded in the day time; the shine of a hoard that he coveted not, and the gleam of the scales of a Dragon that was too loathly for him to battle with

THE DRAGON'S BLOOD

SIGURD went to war: with the men that King Alv gave him he marched into the country that was ruled over by the slayer of his father. The war that he waged was short and the battles that he won were not perilous. Old was King Lygni now, and feeble was his grasp upon his people. Sigurd slew him and took away his treasure and added his lands to the lands of King Alv.

But Sigurd was not content with the victory he had gained. He had dreamt of stark battles and of renown that would be hardily won. What was the war he had waged to the wars that Sigmund his father, and Volsung his father's father, had waged in their days? Not content was Sigurd. He led his men back by the hills from the crests of which he could look upon the Dragon's haunts. And having come as far as those hills he bade his men return to King Alv's hall with the spoils he had won.

They went, and Sigurd stayed upon the hills and looked across Gnita Heath to where Fafnir the Dragon had his lair. All blasted and wasted was the Heath with the fiery breath of the Dragon. And he saw the cave where Fafnir abode, and he saw the track that his comings and goings made. For every day the Dragon left his cave in the cliffs, crossing the Heath to come to the River at which he drank.

For the length of a day Sigurd watched from the hills the haunt of the Dragon. In the evening he saw him lengthening himself out of the cave, and coming on his track across the Heath, in seeming like a ship that travels swiftly because of its many oars.

Then to Regin in his smithy he came. To that cunning man Sigurd said:

"Tell me all thou dost know of Fafnir the Dragon."

Regin began to talk, but his speech was old and strange and filled with runes. When he had spoken it all Sigurd said, "All thou hast told me thou wilt have to say over again in a speech that is known to men of our day."

Then said Regin: "Of a hoard I spoke. The Dwarf Andvari guarded it from the first days of the world. But one of the Æsir forced Andvari to give the hoard to him, masses of gold and heaps of jewels, and the Æsir gave it to Hreidmar, who was my father.

"For the slaying of his son Otter the Æsir gave the

hoard to Hreidmar, the greatest hoard that had ever been seen in the world. But not long was it left to Hreidmar to gloat over. For a son slew a father that he might possess that hoard. Fafnir, that son was Fafnir, my brother.

"Then Fafnir, that no one might disturb his possession of the hoard, turned himself into a Dragon, a Dragon so fearful that none dare come nigh him. And I, Regin, was stricken with covetousness of the hoard. I did not change myself into another being, but, by the magic my father knew, I made my life longer than the generations of men, hoping that I would see Fafnir slain and then have the mighty hoard under my hands.

"Now, son of the Volsungs, thou dost know all that has to do with Fafnir the Dragon, and the great hoard that he guards."

"Little do I care about the hoard he guards," Sigurd said. "I care only that he has made the King's good lands into a waste and that he is an evil thing to men. I would have the renown of slaying Fafnir the Dragon."

"With Gram, the sword thou hast, thou couldst slay Fafnir," Regin cried, his body shaken with his passion for the hoard. "Thou couldst slay him with the sword thou hast. Harken now and I will tell thee how thou mightst give him the deathly stroke through the coils of his mail. Harken, for I have thought of it all.

"The track of the Dragon to the River is broad, for he takes ever the one track. Dig a pit in the middle of that track, and when Fafnir comes over it strike up into his coils of mail with Gram, thy great sword. Gram only may pierce that mail. Then will Fafnir be slain and the hoard will be left guardless."

"What thou sayst is wise, Regin," Sigurd answered. "We will make this pit and I will strike Fafnir in the way thou sayst."

Then Sigurd went and he rode upon Grani, his proud horse, and he showed himself to King Alv and to Hiordis, his mother. Afterwards he went with Regin to the Heath that was the haunt of the Dragon, and in his track they dug a pit for the slaying of Fafnir.

And, lest his horse should scream aloud at the coming of the Dragon, Sigurd had Grani sent back to a cave in the hills. It was Regin that brought Grani away. "I am fearful and can do nothing to help thee, son of the Vol-sungs," he said. "I will go away and await the slaying of Fafnir."

He went, and Sigurd lay down in the pit they had made and practiced thrusting upward with his sword. He lay with his face upward and with his two hands he thrust the mighty sword upward.

But as he lay there he bethought of a dread thing that might happen; namely, that the blood and the venom of the Dragon might pour over him as he lay there, and waste him flesh and bone. When he thought of this Sigurd hastened out of the pit, and he dug other pits near by, and he made a passage for himself from one pit to the other that he might escape from the flow of the Dragon's en-venomed blood.

As he lay down again in the pit he heard the treading of the Dragon and he heard the Dragon's strange and mournful cry. Mightily the Dragon came on and he heard his breathing. His shape came over the pit. Then the Dragon held his head and looked down on Sigurd.

It was the instant for him to make stroke with Gram. He did not let the instant pass. He struck mightily under the shoulder and toward the heart of the beast. The sword went through the hard and glittering scales that were the creature's mail. Sigurd pulled out the sword and drew himself through the passage and out into the second pit as Fafnir's envenomed blood drenched where he had been.

Drawing himself up out of the second pit he saw the huge shape of Fafnir heaving and lashing. He came to him and thrust his sword right through the Dragon's neck. The Dragon reared up as though to fling himself down on Sigurd with all his crushing bulk and dread talons, with his fiery breath and his envenomed blood. But Sigurd leaped aside and ran far off. Then did Fafnir scream his death scream. After he had torn up rocks with his talons he lay prone on the ground, his head in the pit that was filled with his envenomed blood.

Then did Regin, hearing the scream that let him know that Fafnir was slain, come down to where the battle had been fought. When he saw that Sigurd was alive and unharmed he uttered a cry of fury. For his plan had been to have Sigurd drowned and burnt in the pit with the stream of Fafnir's envenomed blood.

But he mastered his fury and showed a pleased countenance to Sigurd. "Now thou wilt have renown," he cried. "Forever wilt thou be called Sigurd, Fafnir's Bane. More renown than ever any of thy fathers had wilt thou have, O Prince of the Volsungs."

So he spoke, saying fair words to him, for now that he was left alive there was something he would have Sigurd do.

"Fafnir is slain," Sigurd said, "and the triumph over him was not lightly won. Now may I show myself to King Alv and to my mother, and the gold from Fafnir's hoard will make me a great spoil."

"Wait," said Regin cunningly. "Wait. Thou hast yet to do something for me. With the sword thou hast, cut through the Dragon and take out his heart for me. When thou hast taken it out, roast it that I may eat of it and become wiser than I am. Do this for me who showed thee how to slay Fafnir."

Sigurd did what Regin would have him do. He cut out the heart of the Dragon and he hung it from stakes to roast. Regin drew away and left him. As Sigurd stood before the fire putting sticks upon it there was a great silence in the forest.

He put his hand down to turn an ashen branch into the heart of the fire. As he did a drop from the roasting Dragon-heart fell upon his hand. The drop burnt into him. He put his hand to his mouth to ease the smart, and his tongue tasted the burning blood of the Dragon.

He went to gather wood for the fire. In a clearing that he came to there were birds; he saw four on a branch together. They spoke to each other in birds' notes, and Sigurd heard and knew what they were saying.

Said the first bird: "How simple is he who has come into this dell! He has no thought of an enemy, and yet he who was with him but a while ago has gone away that he may bring a spear to slay him."

"For the sake of the gold that is in the Dragon's cave he would slay him," said the second bird.

And the third bird said: "If he would eat the Dragon's heart himself he would know all wisdom."

But the fourth bird said: "He has tasted a drop of the Dragon's blood and he knows what we are saying."

The four birds did not fly away nor cease from speaking. Instead they began to tell of a marvelous abode that was known to them.

Deep in the forest, the birds sang, there was a Hall that was called the House of Flame. Its ten walls were Uni, Iri, Barri, Ori, Varns, Vegdrasil, Derri, Uri, Dellinger, Atvarder, and each wall was built by the Dwarf whose name it bore. All round the Hall there was a circle of fire through which none might pass. And within the Hall a maiden slept, and she was the wisest and the bravest and the most beautiful maiden in the world.

Sigurd stood like a man enchanted listening to what the birds sang.

But suddenly they changed the flow of their discourse, and their notes became sharp and piercing.

"Look, look!" cried one. "He is coming against the youth."

"He is coming against the youth with a spear," cried another.

"Now will the youth be slain unless he is swift," cried a third.

Sigurd turned round and he saw Regin treading the way toward him, grim and silent, with a spear in his hands. The spear would have gone through Sigurd had he stayed one instant longer in the place where he had been listening to the speech of the birds. As he turned he had his sword in his hand, and he flung it, and Gram struck Regin on the breast.

Then Regin cried out: "I die — I die without having laid my hands on the hoard that Fafnir guarded. Ah, a curse was upon the hoard, for Hreidmar and Fafnir and I have perished because of it. May the curse of the gold now fall on the one who is my slayer."

Then did Regin breathe out his life. Sigurd took the body and cast it into the pit that was alongside the dead Fafnir. Then, that he might eat the Dragon's heart and become the wisest of men, he went to where he had left it roasting. And he thought that when he had eaten the heart he would go into the Dragon's cave and carry away the treasure that was there, and bring it as spoil of his battle to King Alv and to his mother. Then he would go through the forest and find the House of Flame where slept the maiden who was the wisest and bravest and most beautiful in the world.

But Sigurd did not eat the Dragon's heart. When he came to where he had left it roasting he found that the fire had burnt it utterly.

THE STORY OF SIGMUND AND SIGNY

H E called to Grani, his proud horse; he stood up on a
mound in the Heath and he sent forth a great shout.
And Grani heard in the cave where Regin had left him
and he came galloping to Sigurd with flowing mane and
eyes flashing fire.

He mounted Grani and he rode to Fafnir's cave. When
he went into the place where the Dragon was wont to lie
he saw a door of iron before him. With Gram, his mighty
sword, he hewed through the iron, and with his strong
hands he pulled the door back. Then, before him he saw
the treasure the Dragon guarded, masses of gold and heaps
of shining jewels.

But as he looked on the hoard Sigurd felt some shadow
of the evil that lay over it all. This was the hoard that in

the far-off days the River-Maidens watched over as it lay deep under the flowing water. Then Andvari the Dwarf forced the River-Maidens to give it to him. And Loki had taken it from Andvari, letting loose as he did Gulveig the Witch who had such evil power over the Gods. For the sake of the hoard Fafnir had slain Hreidmar, his father, and Regin had plotted death against Fafnir, his brother.

Not all this history did Sigurd know. But a shadow of its evil touched his spirit as he stood there before the gleaming and glittering heap. He would take all of it away, but not now. The tale that the birds told was in his mind, and the green of the forest was more to him than the glitter of the treasure heap. He would come back with chests and load it up and carry it to King Alv's hall. But first he would take such things as he himself might wear.

He found a helmet of gold and he put it on his head. He found a great armring and he put it around his arm. On the top of the armring there was a small fingerring with a rune graved upon it. Sigurd put it on his finger. And this was the ring that Andvari the Dwarf had put the curse upon when Loki had taken the hoard from him.

He knew that no one would cross the Heath and come to Fafnir's lair, so he did not fear to leave the treasure unguarded. He mounted Grani, his proud horse, and rode toward the forest. He would seek the House of Flame where she lay sleeping, the maiden who was the wisest and the bravest and the most beautiful in the world. With his golden helmet shining above his golden hair Sigurd rode on.

As he rode toward the forest he thought of Sigmund, his father, whose slaying he had avenged, and he thought of Sigmund's father, Volsung, and of the grim deeds that the Volsungs had suffered and wrought.

Rerir, the son of Sigi who was the son of Odin, was the father of Volsung. And Volsung when he was in his first manhood had built his hall around a mighty tree. Its branches went up to the roof and made the beams of the house and its great trunk was the center of the hall. "The Branstock" the tree was called, and Volsung hall was named "The Hall of the Branstock."

Many children had Volsung, eleven sons and one daughter. Strong were all his sons and good fighters, and Volsung of the Hall of the Branstock was a mighty chief.

It was through Signy, the daughter of the house, that a feud and a deadly battle was brought to Volsung and his sons. She was a wise and a fair maiden and her fame went through all the lands. Now, one day Volsung received a message from a King asking for the hand of Signy in marriage. And Volsung who knew of this King through report of his battles sent a message to him saying that he would be welcome to the Hall of the Branstock.

So King Siggeir came with his men. But when the Volsungs looked into his face they liked it not. And Signy shrank away, saying, "This King is evil of heart and false of word."

Volsung and his eleven sons took counsel together. Siggeir had a great force of men with him, and if they refused to give her he could slay them all and harry their kingdom. Besides they had pledged themselves to give Signy when they had sent him a message of welcome. Long counsel they had together. And ten of Signy's brothers said, "Let Signy wed this King. He is not as evil as he seems in her mind." Ten brothers said it. But one spoke out, saying, "We will not give our sister to this evil King. Rather let us all go down fighting with the Hall of the Branstock flaming above our heads."

It was Sigmund, the youngest of the Volsungs, who said this.

But Signy's father said: "We know nought of evil of King Siggeir. Also our word is given to him. Let him feast with us this night in the Hall of the Branstock and let Signy go from us with him as his wife." Then they looked to her and they saw Signy's face and it was white and stern. "Let it be as ye have said, my father and my brothers," she said. "I will wed King Siggeir and go with him overseas." So she said aloud. But Sigmund heard her say to herself, "It is woe for the Volsungs."

A feast was made and King Siggeir and his men came to the Hall of the Branstock. Fires were lighted and tables were spread, and great horns of mead went around the guests. In the middle of the feasting a stranger entered the Hall. He was taller than the tallest there, and his bearing made all do him reverence. One offered him a horn of mead and he drank it. Then, from under the blue cloak that he wore, he drew a sword that made the brightness of the Hall more bright.

He went to the tree that the Hall was built around, to

the Branstock, and he thrust the sword into it. All the company were hushed. Then they heard the voice of the stranger, a voice that was like the trumpet's call: "The sword is for the hand that can draw it out of the Branstock." Then he went out of the Hall.

All looked to where the sword was placed and saw a hand's breadth of wonderful brightness. This one and that one would have laid hands on the hilt, only Volsung's voice bade them stand still. "It is meet," he said, "that our guest and our son-in-law, King Siggeir, should be the first to put hands on its hilt and try to draw the sword of the stranger out of the Branstock."

King Siggeir went to the tree and laid his hands on the broad hilt. He strove hard to draw out the sword, but all his might could not move it. As he strained himself to draw it and failed, a dark look of anger came into his face.

Then others tried to draw it, the captains who were with King Siggeir, and they, too, failed to move the blade. Then Volsung tried and Volsung could not move it. One after the other, his eleven sons strained to draw out the stranger's sword. At last it came to the turn of the youngest, to Sigmund, to try. And when Sigmund laid his hand on the broad hilt and drew it, behold! The sword came with his hand, and once again the Hall was brightened with its marvelous brightness.

It was a wondrous sword, a sword made out of better metal and by smiths more cunning than any known. All envied Sigmund that he had won for himself that wonder-weapon.

King Siggeir looked on it with greedy eyes. "I will give thee its weight in gold for that sword, good brother," he said.

But Sigmund said to him proudly: "If the sword was for thy hand thou shouldst have won it. The sword was not for thine, but for a Volsung's hand."

And Signy, looking at King Siggeir, saw a look of deeper evil come into his face. She knew that hatred for all the Volsung race was in his heart.

But at the end of the feast she was wed to King Siggeir, and the next day she left the Hall of the Branstock and went with him down to where his great painted ship was drawn up on the beach. And when they were parting from her, her father and her brothers, King Siggeir invited them to come to his country, as friends visiting friends and kinsmen visiting kinsmen, and look on Signy again. And he stood on the beach and would not go on board his ship until each and all of the Volsungs gave their word that they would visit Signy and him in his own land. "And when thou comest," he said to Sigmund, "be sure thou dost bring with thee the mighty sword that thou didst win."

All this was thought of by Sigurd, the son of Sigmund, as he rode toward the fringe of the forest.

The time came for Volsung and his sons to redeem the promise they made to King Siggeir. They made ready their ship and they sailed from the land where stood the Hall of the Branstock. And they landed on the coast of King Siggeir's country, and they drew their ship up on the beach and they made their camp there, intending to come to the King's Hall in the broad light of the day.

But in the half light of the dawn one came to the Volsung ship. A cloak and hood covered the figure, but Sigmund, who was the watcher, knew who it was. "Signy!" he said, and Signy asked that her father and her brothers be awakened until she would speak to them of a treason that was brewed against them.

"King Siggeir has made ready a great army against your coming," she told them. "He hates the Volsungs, the branch as well as the root, and it is his plan to fall upon you, my father and my brothers, with his great army and slay you all. And he would possess himself of Gram, Sigmund's wonder-sword. Therefore, I say to you, O Volsungs, draw your ship into the sea and sail from the land where such treachery can be."

But Volsung, her father, would not listen. "The Volsungs do not depart like broken men from a land they have brought their ship to," he said. "We gave, each and all, the word that we would visit King Siggeir and visit him we will. And if he is a dastard and would fall upon us, why we are the unbeaten Volsungs, and we will fight against him and his army and slay him, and bear you back with us to the Hall of the Branstock. The day widens now, and we shall go to the Hall."

Signy would have spoken of the great army King Siggeir had gathered, but she knew that the Volsungs never harkened to talk of odds. She spoke no more, but bowed her head and went back to King Siggeir's hall.

Siggeir knew that Signy had been to warn her father and her brothers. He called the men he had gathered and he posted them cunningly in the way the Volsungs would come. Then he sent one to the ship with a message of welcome.

As they left their ship the army of King Siggeir fell upon the Volsungs and their followers. Very fierce was the battle that was waged on the beach, and many and many a one of King Siggeir's fierce fighters went down before the fearless ones that made Volsung's company. But at last Volsung himself was slain and his eleven sons were taken captive. And Gram, his mighty sword, was taken out of Sigmund's hands.

They were brought before King Siggeir in his hall, the eleven Volsung princes. Siggeir laughed to see them before him. "Ye are not in the Hall of the Branstock now, to dishonor me with black looks and scornful words," he said, "and a harder task will be given you than that of drawing a sword out of a tree-trunk. Before set of sun I will see you hewn to pieces with the sword."

Then Signy who was there stood up with her white face and her wide eyes, and she said: "I pray not for longer life for my brothers, for well I know that my prayers would avail them nought. But dost thou not heed the proverb, Siggeir — 'Sweet to the eye as long as the eye can see'?"

And Siggeir laughed his evil laugh when he heard her. "Aye, my Queen," he said, "sweet to the eye as long as the eye may see their torments. They shall not die at once nor all together. I will let them see each other die."

So Siggeir gave a new order to his dastard troops. The order was that the eleven brothers should be taken into the depths of the forest and chained to great beams and left there. This was done with the eleven sons of Volsung.

The next day one who had watched and who was faithful to Signy came, and Signy said to him: "What has befallen my brothers?"

And the watcher said: "A great wolf came to where the chained men are, and fell upon the first of them and devoured him."

When Signy heard this no tears came from her eyes, but that which was hard around her heart became harder. She said, "Go again, and watch what befalls."

And the watcher came the second time and said: "The second of your brothers has been devoured by the wolf." Signy shed no tears this time either, and again that which was hard around her heart became harder.

And every day the watcher came and he told her what had befallen her brothers. And it came to the time when but one of her brothers was left alive, Sigmund, the youngest.

Then said Signy: "Not without device are we left at the end. I have thought of what is to be done. Take a pot of honey to where he is chained and smear Sigmund's face with the honey."

The watcher did as Signy bade him.

Again the great wolf came along the forest-ways to where Sigmund was chained. When she snuffed over him she found the honey upon his face. She put down her

tongue to lick over his face. Then, with his strong teeth
Sigmund seized the tongue of the wolf. She fought and she
struggled with all her might, but Sigmund did not let go
of her tongue. The struggle with the beast broke the beam
to which he was chained. Then Sigmund seized the wolf
with his hands and tore her jaws apart.

The watcher saw this happening and told of it to Signy.
A fierce joy went through her, and she said: "One of the
Volsungs lives, and vengeance will be wrought upon King
Siggeir and upon his house."

Still the watcher stayed in the ways of the forest, and he
marked where Sigmund built for himself a hidden hut.
Often he bore tokens from Signy to Sigmund. Sigmund
took to the ways of the hunter and the outlaw, but he did
not forsake the forest. And King Siggeir knew not that
one of the Volsungs lived and was near him.

THE STORY OF SIGMUND
AND SINFIOTLI

AS Sigurd rode the ways of the forest he thought upon
Sigmund, his father, on his life and his death, according to what Hiordis, his mother, had told him. Sigmund
lived for long the life of the hunter and the outlaw, but
he never strayed far from the forest that was in King Siggeir's dominion. Often did he get a token from Signy.
They two, the last of the Volsungs, knew that King Siggeir
and his house would have to perish for the treason he had
wrought on their father and their brothers.

Sigmund knew that his sister would send her son to help
him. One morning there came to his hut a boy of ten years.
He knew that this was one of Signy's sons, and that she

would have him train him into being a warrior worthy of the Volsung breed.

Sigmund hardly looked and hardly spoke to the lad. He was going hunting, and as he took down his spear from the wall he said:

"There is the mealbag, boy. Mix the meal and make the bread, and we will eat when I come back."

When he returned the bread was unmade, and the boy was standing watching the mealbag with widened eyes. "Thou didst not make the bread?" Sigmund said.

"Nay," said the boy, "I was afeard to go near the bag. Something stirred within it."

"Thou hast the heart of a mouse so to be frighted. Go back to thy mother and tell her that not in thee is the stuff for a Volsung warrior."

So Sigmund spoke, and the boy went away weeping.

A year later another son of Signy's came. As before Sigmund hardly looked at and hardly spoke to the boy. He said:

"There is the mealbag. Mix the meal and make ready the bread against the time I return."

When Sigmund came back the bread was unmade. The boy had shrunk away from where the bag was.

"Thou hast not made the bread?" Sigmund said.

"Nay," said the boy, "something stirred in the bag, and I was afeard."

"Thou hast the heart of a mouse. Get thee back to thy mother and tell her that there is not in thee the stuff for the making of a Volsung warrior."

And this boy, like his brother, went back weeping.

At that time Signy had no other sons. But at last one was born to her, the child of a desperate thought. Him, too, when he was grown, she sent to Sigmund.

"What did thy mother say to thee?" Sigmund said to this boy when he showed himself at the hut.

"Nothing. She sewed my gloves to my hands and then bade me pull them off."

"And didst thou?"

"Aye, and the skin came with them."

"And didst thou weep?"

"A Volsung does not weep for such a thing."

Long did Sigmund look on the lad. He was tall and fair and great-limbed, and his eyes had no fear in them.

"What wouldst thou have me do for thee?" said the lad.

"There is the mealbag," Sigmund said. "Mix the meal and make the bread for me against the time I return."

When Sigmund came back the bread was baking on the coals. "What didst thou with the meal?" Sigmund asked.

"I mixed it. Something was in the meal — a serpent, I think — but I kneaded it with the meal, and now the serpent is baking on the coals."

Sigmund laughed and threw his arms around the boy. "Thou wilt not eat of that bread," he said. "Thou didst knead into it a venomous serpent."

The boy's name was Sinfiotli. Sigmund trained him in the ways of the hunter and the outlaw. Here and there they went, taking vengeance on King Siggeir's men. The boy was fierce, but never did he speak a word that was false.

One day when Sigmund and Sinfiotli were hunting,

they came upon a strange house in the dark wood. When they went within they found two men lying there sleeping a deep sleep. On their arms were heavy rings of gold, and Sigmund knew that they were the sons of Kings.

And beside the sleeping men he saw wolfskins, left there as though they had been cast off. Then Sigmund knew that these men were shape-changers — that they were ones who changed their shapes and ranged through the forests as wolves.

Sigmund and Sinfiotli put on the skins that the men had cast off, and when they did this they changed their shapes and became as wolves. And as wolves they ranged through the forest, now and then changing their shapes back to those of men. As wolves they fell upon King Siggeir's men and slew more and more of them.

One day Sigmund said to Sinfiotli: "Thou art still young and I would not have thee be too rash. If thou dost come upon a company of seven men, fight them. But if thou dost come on a company greater than seven, raise up thy voice as a wolf's cry and bring me to thy side."

Sinfiotli promised that he would do this.

One day, as he went through the forest in his wolf's shape, Sigmund heard the din of a struggle and he stopped to listen for Sinfiotli's call. But no call came. Then Sigmund went through the forest in the direction of the struggle. On his way he passed the bodies of eleven slain men. And he came upon Sinfiotli lying in the thicket, his wolf's shape upon him, and panting from the battle he had waged.

"Thou didst strive with eleven men. Why didst thou not call to me?" Sigmund said.

"Why should I have called to thee? I am not so feeble but I can strive with eleven men."

Sigmund was made angry with this answer. He looked on Sinfiotli where he lay, and the wicked wolf's nature that was in the skin came over him. He sprang upon him, sinking his teeth in Sinfiotli's throat.

Sinfiotli lay gasping in the throes of death. And Sigmund, knowing the deadly grip that was in those jaws of his, howled his anguish.

Then, as he licked the face of his comrade, he saw two weasels meet. They began to fight, one with the other, and the first caught the second at the throat, and bit him with his teeth and laid him out as if in death. Sigmund marked the combat and the end of it. But then the first weasel ran and found leaves of a certain herb and he put them upon his comrade's wound. And the herb cured the wound, and the weasel that was bitten rose up and was sound and swift again.

Sigmund went searching for the herb he saw the weasel carry to his comrade. And as he sought for it he saw a raven with a leaf in her beak. She dropped the leaf as he came to her, and behold! It was the same leaf as the weasel had brought to his comrade. Sigmund took it and laid it on the wound he had made in Sinfiotli's throat, and the wound healed, and Sinfiotli was sound once more. They went back to their hut in the forest. And the next day they burnt the wolfskins, and they prayed the Gods that they might never be afflicted with the wolf's evil nature again. And Sigmund and Sinfiotli never afterwards changed their shapes.

THE STORY OF THE VENGEANCE
OF THE VOLSUNGS AND OF
THE DEATH OF SINFIOTLI

AND now Sinfiotli had come to his full strength and it was time to take vengeance on King Siggeir for the slaying of Volsung and the dread doom he had set for Volsung's ten sons. Sigmund and Sinfiotli put helmets on their heads and took swords in their hands and went to King Siggeir's Hall. They hid behind the casks of ale that were at the entrance and they waited for the men-at-arms to leave the Hall that they might fall upon King Siggeir and his attendants.

The younger children of King Siggeir were playing in the Hall and one let fall a ball. It went rolling behind the casks of ale. And the child peering after the ball saw two men crouching with swords in their hands and helmets on their heads.

The child told a servant who told the King. Then Siggeir arose, and he drew his men-at-arms around him, and he set them on the men who were hiding behind the barrels. Sigmund and Sinfiotli sprang up and fought against the men of King Siggeir, but they were taken captives.

Now they might not be slain there and then, for it was unlawful to slay captives after sunset. But for all that, King Siggeir would not leave them above ground. He decreed that they should be put in a pit, and a mound made over them so that they would be buried alive.

The sentence was carried out. A great flagstone was put down to divide the pit in two, so that Sigmund and Sinfiotli might hear each other's struggle and not be able to give help to each other. All was done as the King commanded.

But while his thralls were putting sods over the pit, one came amongst them, cloaked and hooded, and dropped something wrapped in straw into the side of the pit where Sinfiotli lay. And when the sky was shut out from them with the turf and soil that was put over the pit, Sinfiotli shouted to Sigmund: "I shall not die, for the queen has thrown down to me meat wrapped in a parcel of straw."

And a while afterwards Sinfiotli shouted to Sigmund: "The queen has left a sword in the meat which she flung down to me. It is a mighty sword. Almost I think it is Gram, the sword you told me of."

"If it be Gram," Sigmund said, "it is a sword that can

cut through this flagstone. Thrust the blade against the stone and try."

Sinfiotli thrust the blade against the stone and the blade went through the stone. Then, one on each side, they took hold of the sword and they cut the great stone in two. Afterwards, working together, it was easy to shift the turf and soil. The two came out under the sky.

Before them was the Hall of King Siggeir. They came to the Hall and they set dry wood before it and they fired the wood and made the Hall blaze up. And when the Hall was in a blaze King Siggeir came to the door and shouted, "Who is it that has fired the house of the King?"

And Sigmund said, "I, Sigmund, the son of Volsung, that you may pay for the treason wrought on the Volsungs."

Seeing Sigmund there with Gram, the great sword, in his hands, Siggeir went back into his Hall. Then Signy was seen with her white face and her stern eyes, and Sigmund called to her, "Come forth, come forth. Sigmund calls. Come out of Siggeir's blazing house and together we will go back to the Hall of the Branstock."

But Signy said, "All is finished now. The vengeance is wrought and I have no more to keep me in life. The Volsung race lives on in you, my brother, and that is my joy. Not merrily did I wed King Siggeir and not merrily did I live with him, but merrily will I die with him now."

She went within the Hall; then the flames burst over it and all who were within perished. Thus the vengeance of the Volsungs was wrought.

And Sigurd thought on the deed that Sigmund, his

father, and Sinfiotli, the youth who was his father's kinsman, wrought, as he rode the ways of the forest, and of the things that thereafter befell them.

Sigmund and Sinfiotli left King Siggeir's land and came back to the land where was the Hall of the Branstock. Sigmund became a great King and Sinfiotli was the Captain of his host.

And the story of Sigmund and Sinfiotli goes on to tell how Sigmund wed a woman whose name was Borghild, and how Sinfiotli loved a woman who was loved by Borghild's brother. A battle came in which the youths were on opposite sides, and Sinfiotli killed Borghild's brother, and it was in fair combat.

Sinfiotli returned home. To make peace between him and the Queen, Sigmund gave Borghild a great measure of gold as compensation for the loss of her brother. The Queen took it and said, "Lo, my brother's worth is reckoned at this; let no more be said about his slaying." And she made Sinfiotli welcome to the Hall of the Branstock.

But although she showed herself friendly to him her heart was set upon his destruction.

That night there was a feast in the Hall of the Branstock and Borghild the Queen went to all the guests with a horn of mead in her hand. She came to Sinfiotli and she held the horn to him. "Take this from my hands, O friend of Sigmund," she said.

But Sinfiotli saw what was in her eyes and he said, "I will not drink from this horn. There is venom in the drink."

Then, to end the mockery that the Queen would have made over Sinfiotli, Sigmund who was standing by took the horn out of Borghild's hand. No venom or poison could injure him. He raised the horn to his lips and drained the mead at a draught.

The Queen said to Sinfiotli, "Must other men quaff thy drink for thee?"

Later in the night she came to him again, the horn of mead in her hand. She offered it to Sinfiotli, but he looked in her eyes and saw the hatred that was there. "Venom is in the drink," he said. "I will not take it."

And again Sigmund took the horn and drank the mead at a draught. And again the Queen mocked Sinfiotli.

A third time she came to him. Before she offered the horn she said, "This is the one who fears to take his drink like a man. What a Volsung heart he has!" Sinfiotli saw the hatred in her eyes, and her mockery could not make him take the mead from her. As before Sigmund was standing by. But now he was weary of raising the horn and he said to Sinfiotli, "Pour the drink through thy beard."

He thought that Sigmund meant that he should pour the mead through his lips that were bearded and make trouble no more between him and the Queen. But Sigmund did not mean that. He meant that he should pretend to drink and let the mead run down on the floor. Sinfiotli, not understanding what his comrade meant, took the horn from the Queen and raised it to his lips and drank. And as soon as he drank, the venom that was in the drink went to his heart, and he fell dead in the Hall of the Branstock.

Oh, woeful was Sigmund for the death of his kinsman and his comrade. He would let no one touch his body. He himself lifted Sinfiotli in his arms and carried him out of the Hall, and through the wood, and down to the seashore. And when he came to the shore he saw a boat drawn up with a man therein. Sigmund came near to him and saw that the man was old and strangely tall. "I will take thy burthen from thee," the man said.

Sigmund left the body of Sinfiotli in the boat, thinking to take a place beside it. But as soon as the body was placed in it the boat went from the land without sail or oars. Sigmund, looking on the old man who stood at the stern, knew that he was not of mortal men, but was Odin All-Father, the giver of the sword Gram.

Then Sigmund went back to his Hall. His Queen died, and in time he wed with Hiordis, who became the mother of Sigurd. And now Sigurd the Volsung, the son of Sigmund and Hiordis, rode the ways of the forest, the sword Gram by his side, and the Golden Helmet of the Dragon's Hoard above his golden hair.

BRYNHILD IN THE HOUSE
OF FLAME

THE forest ways led him on and up a mountain-side.
He came to a mountain-summit at last: Hindfell,
where the trees fell away, leaving a place open to the sky
and the winds. On Hindfell was the House of Flame.
Sigurd saw the walls black, and high, and all around them
was a ring of fire.

As he rode nearer he heard the roar of the mounting
and the circling fire. He sat on Grani, his proud horse,
and for long he looked on the black walls and the flame
that went circling around them.

Then he rode Grani to the fire. Another horse would
have been affrighted, but Grani remained steady under

Sigurd. To the wall of fire they came, and Sigurd, who knew no fear, rode through it.

Now he was in the courtyard of the Hall. No stir was there of man or hound or horse. Sigurd dismounted and bade Grani be still. He opened a door and he saw a chamber with hangings on which was wrought the pattern of a great tree, a tree with three roots, and the pattern was carried across from one wall to the other. On a couch in the center of the chamber one lay in slumber. Upon the head was a helmet and across the breast was a breastplate. Sigurd took the helmet off the head. Then over the couch fell a heap of woman's hair — wondrous, bright-gleaming hair. This was the maiden that the birds had told him of.

He cut the fastenings of the breastplate with his sword, and he gazed long upon her. Beautiful was her face, but stern; like the face of one who subdues but may not be subdued. Beautiful and strong were her arms and her hands. Her mouth was proud, and over her closed eyes there were strong and beautiful brows.

Her eyes opened, and she turned them and looked full upon Sigurd. "Who art thou who hast awakened me?" she said.

"I am Sigurd, the son of Sigmund, of the Volsung race," he answered.

"And thou didst ride through the ring of fire to me?"

"That did I."

She knelt on the couch and stretched out her arms to where the light shone. "Hail, O Day," she cried, "and hail, O beams that are the sons of Day. O Night, and O daughter of Night, may ye look on us with eyes that bless. Hail, O Æsir and O Asyniur! Hail, O wide-spreading fields of Midgard! May ye give us wisdom, and wise speech, and healing power, and grant that nothing untrue or unbrave may come near us!"

All this she cried with eyes open wide; they were eyes that had in them all the blue that Sigurd had ever seen: the blue of flowers, the blue of skies, the blue of battle-blades. She turned those great eyes upon him and she said, "I am Brynhild, once a Valkyrie but now a mortal maiden, one who will know death and all the sorrows that mortal women know. But there are things that I may not know, things that are false and of no bravery."

She was the bravest and the wisest and the most beautiful maiden in the world: Sigurd knew that it was so. He laid his sword Gram at her feet, and he said her name, "Brynhild." He told her how he had slain the Dragon, and how he had heard the birds tell of her. She rose from the couch and bound her wondrous hair on her head. In wonder he watched her. When she moved it was as though she walked above the earth.

They sat together and she told him wonderful and secret things. And she told him, too, how she was sent by Odin from Asgard to choose the slain for his hall Valhalla, and to give victory to those whom he willed to have it. And she told how she had disobeyed the will of All-Father, and how for that she was made outcast of Asgard. Odin put into her flesh the thorn of the Tree of Sleep that she might remain in slumber until one who was the bravest of mortal men should waken her. Whoever would break the fastenings of the breastplate would take out the Thorn of Sleep. "Odin granted me this," she said, "that as a mortal maid I should wed none but him who is the bravest in the world. And so that none but him might come to me, All-Father put the fire-ring round where I lay in slumber. And it is thou, Sigurd, son of Sigmund, who hast come to me. Thou art the bravest and I think thou art the most beautiful too; like to Tyr, the God who wields the sword."

She told him that whoever rode through the fire and claimed her as his wife, him she must wed.

They talked to each other fondly and the day flowed by them. Then Sigurd heard Grani, his horse, neigh for him again and again. He cried to Brynhild: "Let me go from the gaze of thine eyes. I am that one who is to have the greatest name in the world. Not yet have I made my name as great as my father and my father's father made their names great. I have overcome King Lygni, and I have slain Fafnir the Dragon, but that is little. I would make my name the greatest in the world, and endure all that is to be endured in making it so. Then I would come back to thee in the House of Flame."

Brynhild said to him: "Well dost thou speak. Make thy name great, and endure what thou hast to endure in making it so. I will wait for thee, knowing that none but Sigurd will be able to win through the fire that guards where I abide."

They gazed long on each other, but little more they spoke. Then they held each other's hands in farewell, and they plighted faith, promising each other that they would take no other man or maiden for their mate. And for token of their troth Sigurd took the ring that was on his finger and placed it on Brynhild's — Andvari's ring it was.

SIGURD AT THE HOUSE OF
THE NIBELUNGS

HE left Hindfell and he came into a kingdom that was
ruled over by a people that were called the Nibelungs as Sigurd's people were called the Volsungs. Giuki
was the name of the King of that land.

Giuki and his Queen and all their sons gave a great
welcome to Sigurd when he came to their hall, for he
looked such a one as might win the name of being the
world's greatest hero. And Sigurd went to war beside the
King's sons, Gunnar and Högni, and the three made
great names for themselves, but Sigurd's shone high above
the others.

When they came back from that war there were great
rejoicings in the hall of the Nibelungs, and Sigurd's heart

was filled with friendship for all the Nibelung race; he had love for the King's sons, Gunnar and Högni, and with Gunnar and Högni he swore oaths of brotherhood. Henceforward he and they would be as brethren. King Giuki had a stepson named Guttorm and he was not bound in the oath that bound Sigurd and the others in brotherhood.

After the war they had waged Sigurd spent a whole winter in the hall of the Nibelungs. His heart was full of memories of Brynhild and of longings to ride to her in the House of Flame and to take her with him to the kingdom that King Giuki would have given him. But as yet he would not go back to her, for he had sworn to give his brethren further help.

One day, as he rode by himself, he heard birds talk to each other and he knew the words they were saying. One said, "There is Sigurd who wears the wondrous helmet that he took out of Fafnir's hoard." And the other bird said, "He knows not that by that helmet he can change his shape as Fafnir changed his shape, and make him look like this creature or that creature, or this man or that man." And the third bird said, "He knows not that the helmet can do anything so wonderful for him."

He rode back to the hall of the Nibelungs, and at the supperboard he told them what he had heard the birds say. He showed them the wondrous helmet. Also he told them how he had slain Fafnir the Dragon, and of how he had won the mighty hoard for himself. His two sworn brothers who were there rejoiced that he had such wondrous possessions.

But more precious than the hoard and more wondrous than the helmet was the memory of Brynhild that he had. But of this he said no word.

Grimhild was the name of the Queen. She was the mother of Gunnar and Högni and their half-brother Guttorm. And she and the King had one daughter whose name was Gudrun. Now Grimhild was one of the wisest of women, and she knew when she looked upon him that Sigurd was the world's greatest warrior. She would have him belong to the Nibelungs, not only by the oaths of brotherhood he had sworn with Gunnar and Högni, but by other ties. And when she heard of the great hoard that was his she had greater wish and will that he should be one with the Nibelungs. She looked on the helmet of gold and on the great armring that he wore, and she made it her heart's purpose that Sigurd should wed with Gudrun, her daughter. But neither Sigurd nor the maiden Gudrun knew of Grimhild's resolve.

And the Queen, watching Sigurd closely, knew that he had a remembrance in his breast that held him from seeing Gudrun's loveliness. She had knowledge of spells and secret brews (she was of the race of Borghild whose brew had destroyed Sinfiotli's life) and she knew that she could make a potion that would destroy the memory Sigurd held.

She mixed the potion. Then one night when there was feasting in the hall of the Nibelungs, she gave the cup that held the potion into the hands of Gudrun and bade her carry it to Sigurd.

Sigurd took the cup out of the hands of the fair Nibelung maiden and he drank the potion. When he had drunk it he put the cup down and he stood amongst the feasters like a man in a dream. And like a man in a dream he went into his chamber, and for a day and a night afterwards he was silent and his mind was astray. When he rode out with Gunnar and Högni they would say to him, "What is it thou hast lost, brother?" Sigurd could not tell them. But what he had lost was all memory of Brynhild the Valkyrie in the House of Flame.

He saw Gudrun and it was as though he looked upon her for the first time. Soft were the long tresses of her hair; soft were her hands. Her eyes were like woodflowers, and her ways and her speech were gentle. Yet was she noble in her bearing as became a Princess who would come into a kingdom. And from the first time she had seen him upon Grani, his proud horse, and with his golden helmet above his golden hair, Gudrun had loved Sigurd.

At the season when the wild swans came to the lake Gudrun went down to watch them build their nests. And while she was there Sigurd rode through the pines. He saw her, and her beauty made the whole place change. He stopped his horse and listened to her voice as she sang to the wild swans, sang the song that Völund made for Alvit, his swan-bride.

No more was Sigurd's heart empty of memory: it was filled with the memory of Gudrun as he saw her by the lake when the wild swans were building their nests. And now he watched her in the hall, sitting with her mother embroidering, or serving her father or her brothers, and tenderness for the maiden kept growing in his heart.

A day came when he asked Gunnar and Högni, his sworn brethren, for Gudrun. They were glad as though a great fortune had befallen them. And they brought him before Giuki the King, and Grimhild the Queen. It seemed as if they had cast off all trouble and care and entered into the prime of their life and power, so greatly did the King and the Queen rejoice at Sigurd's becoming one with the Nibelungs through his marriage with Gudrun.

When Gudrun heard that Sigurd had asked for her, she said to the Queen: "Oh, my mother, your wisdom should have strengthened me to bear such joy. How can I show him that he is so dear, so dear to me? But I shall try not to show it, for he might deem that there was no sense in me but sense to love him. So great a warrior would not care for such love. I would be with him as a battle-maiden."

Sigurd and Gudrun were wed and all the kingdom that the Nibelungs ruled over rejoiced. And Queen Grimhild thought that though the effect of the potion she gave would wear away, his love for Gudrun would ever fill his heart, and that no other memory would be able to find a place there.

HOW BRYNHILD WAS WON
FOR GUNNAR

NOW that Sigurd had wed Gudrun he was one with the Nibelungs. The hoard that was in Fafnir's cave he brought away and he left it in their treasure house. He went into his fosterfather's kingdom again, and he saw King Alv and Hiordis, his mother. But he had no memory now of the House of Flame, nor of Brynhild, who waited there for him.

King Giuki died, and Gunnar, Sigurd's sworn brother, became King in his stead. His mother would have him wed, but Gunnar told her he had seen no maiden whom he would choose for his wife.

But when Sigurd and he were together Gunnar would speak of a maiden far away, one whom he often thought on. And one day when Sigurd pressed him to tell who this maiden was, he spoke of one whom the wisest of the poets told of, a maiden in a Hall with a flame around it, a maiden named Brynhild who was guarded by a ring of fire.

Sigurd laughed to think that his shrewd brother was beguiled by one whom he had only heard of. But if he was beguiled by the tale of her, why should he not come to her and wed her? So Sigurd said. Then Gunnar bent to him and asked Sigurd would he aid him to win her? And Sigurd took Gunnar's hand and swore that he would.

So they started off for Hindfell, Gunnar and Högni and Sigurd. They rode on until they came in sight of the black walls with the mounting and circling fire around them. No memory had Sigurd of the place. With the flame of eagerness upon his stolid face Gunnar went forward to ride through the ring of fire. He brought Goti, his horse, near the flame, but the horse, for no urging, would go through it. Then Gunnar thought that, mounted on Grani, Sigurd's horse, he could ride through the ring of fire. He mounted Grani and came near to the flaring wall. But Grani, knowing that the one who rode him had fear of the fire, reared up and would not go through it. Only with Sigurd on his back would Grani go through the flame.

Then were the three sworn brethren greatly discomfited. But after they had considered it for long Högni the Wise said: "There is a way to win Brynhild, and that is for Sigurd to change shapes, by the magic of his helmet, with Gunnar. Then Sigurd could ride Grani through the wall of flame and come to Brynhild in Gunnar's shape."

So spoke Högni the Wise, and when he saw his sworn brother's gaze fixed on him in pleading, Sigurd could not but agree to ride through the flame and come to Brynhild in the way he said. And so by the magic of his helmet he changed shapes with Gunnar. Then he mounted Grani and rode to the wall of flame. And Grani, knowing that the one he bore was without fear, rode through the flaring fire. Then Sigurd came into the courtyard of the House of Flame. He dismounted from Grani, and he bade his horse be still.

He went within the Hall and he saw one with a bow in her hands shooting at a mark. She turned to him, and he saw a beautiful and stern face, with coils of wondrous, bright-gleaming hair and eyes that were like stars in an unventured-in sea. He thought that the arrow in her hands had been shot through him. But it was not so. Brynhild threw down the bow and came to him with that walk of hers that was as of one moving above the earth. And when she came near and looked upon him she uttered a strange cry.

"Who art thou?" she said. "Who art thou who hast come to me through the wall of flaring fire?"

"Gunnar, son of Giuki, of the race of the Nibelungs," Sigurd said.

"Art thou the bravest one in the world?" she asked.

"I have ridden through the wall of flaring fire to come to thee," Sigurd answered.

"He who has come through that wall of flaring fire may claim me," Brynhild said. "It is written in the runes, and it must be so. But I thought there was only one who would come to me through it." She looked at him, and her eyes had a flame of anger. "Oh, I would strive with thee with warrior-weapons," she cried. Then Sigurd felt her strong hands upon him, and he knew that she was striving to throw him.

They wrestled, and each was so strong that none could move the other. They wrestled, Sigurd the first of heroes, and Brynhild, the Valkyrie. Sigurd got her hand in his in the wrestle. On that hand was a ring, and Sigurd bent back the finger and drew it off.

It was Andvari's ring, the ring he had placed on her finger. And when the ring was taken off it, Brynhild sank down on her knees like one that was strengthless.

Then Sigurd lifted her in his arms and carried her to where Grani, his horse, was waiting. He lifted her across his horse, and he mounted behind her and again he rode through the wall of flame. Högni and Gunnar were waiting, Gunnar in Sigurd's shape. Brynhild did not look upon them, but covered her face with her hands. Then Sigurd took back his own shape, and he rode before Gunnar and Högni to the hall of the Nibelungs.

He went within, and he found Gudrun, his wife, playing with Sigmund, his little son, and he sat beside her and he told her of all that had befallen: how, for the sake of the sworn brotherhood, he had won Brynhild the Valkyrie for Gunnar, and how he had striven with her and had overcome her, and had taken off her finger the ring that he now wore upon his own.

And even as he spoke to his wife the fume of the potion that Gudrun's mother had given him was wearing off, and he had memories of going to the House of Flame on a day that was not this day, and of riding through the wall of fire in his own shape. And again, as on the night when he drank the potion that Queen Grimhild brewed, he became as one whose wits are astray. He stood watching his child as he played, and his wife as she worked at her embroidery, and he was as a man in a dream.

While he was standing there Gunnar and Högni came into the hall of the Nibelungs bringing Brynhild with them. Gudrun rose up to welcome her who came as her brother's bride. Then did Sigurd look on Brynhild and then did he remember all. And when he remembered all such a mighty sigh rose from his heart as burst the links of the mail that was across his breast.

THE DEATH OF SIGURD

IT happened one day that Brynhild, Gunnar's wife, now
a Queen, was with Sigurd's wife, bathing in a river.
Not often they were together. Brynhild was the haughtiest
of women, and often she treated Gudrun with disdain.
Now as they were bathing together, Gudrun, shaking out
her hair, cast some drops upon Brynhild. Brynhild went
from Gudrun. And Sigurd's wife, not knowing that Brynhild had anger against her, went after her up the stream.

"Why dost thou go so far up the river, Brynhild?"
Gudrun asked.

"So that thou mayst not shake thy hair over me," answered Brynhild.

Gudrun stood still while Brynhild went up the river

like a creature who was made to be alone. "Why dost thou speak so to me, sister?" Gudrun cried.

She remembered that from the first Brynhild had been haughty with her, often speaking to her with harshness and bitterness. She did not know what cause Brynhild had for this.

It was because Brynhild had seen in Sigurd the one who had ridden through the fire for the first time, he who had awakened her by breaking the binding of her breast-plate and so drawing out of her flesh the thorn of the Tree of Sleep. She had given him her love when she awakened on the world. But he, as she thought, had forgotten her easily, giving his love to this other maiden. Brynhild, with her Valkyrie's pride, was left with a mighty anger in her heart.

"Why dost thou speak so to me, Brynhild?" Gudrun asked.

"It would be ill indeed if drops from thy hair fell on one who is so much above thee, one who is King Gunnar's wife," Brynhild answered.

"Thou art married to a King, but not to one more valorous than my lord," Gudrun said.

"Gunnar is more valorous; why dost thou compare Sigurd with him?" Brynhild said.

"He slew the Dragon Fafnir, and won for himself Fafnir's hoard," said Gudrun.

"Gunnar rode through the ring of fire. Mayhap thou wilt tell us that Sigurd did the like," said Brynhild.

"Yea," said Gudrun, now made angry. "It was Sigurd

and not Gunnar who rode through the ring of fire. He rode through it in Gunnar's shape, and he took the ring off thy finger — look, it is now on mine."

And Gudrun held out her hand on which was Andvari's ring. Then Brynhild knew, all at once, that what Gudrun said was true. It was Sigurd that rode through the ring of fire the second as well as the first time. It was he who had struggled with her, taking the ring off her hand and claiming her for a bride, not for himself but for another, and out of disdain.

Falsely had she been won. And she, one of Odin's Valkyries, had been wed to one who was not the bravest hero in the world, and she to whom untruth might not come had been deceived. She was silent now, and all the pride that was in her turned to hatred of Sigurd.

She went to Gunnar, her husband, and she told him that she was so deeply shamed that she could never be glad in his Hall again; that never would he see her drinking wine, nor embroidering with golden threads, and never would he hear her speaking words of kindness. And when she said this to him she rent the web she was weaving, and she wept aloud so that all in the hall heard her, and all marveled to hear the proud Queen cry.

Then Sigurd came to her, and he offered in atonement the whole hoard of Fafnir. And he told her how forgetfulness of her had come upon him, and he begged her to forgive him for winning her in falseness. But she answered him: "Too late thou hast come to me, Sigurd. Now I have only a great anger in my heart."

When Gunnar came she told him she would forgive him, and love him as she had not loved him before, if he would slay Sigurd. But Gunnar would not slay him, although Brynhild's passion moved him greatly, since Sigurd was a sworn brother of his.

Then she went to Högni and asked him to slay Sigurd, telling him that the whole of Fafnir's hoard would belong to the Nibelungs if Sigurd were slain. But Högni would not slay him, since Sigurd and he were sworn brothers.

There was one who had not sworn brotherhood with Sigurd. He was Guttorm, Gunnar's and Högni's half-brother. Brynhild went to Guttorm. He would not slay Sigurd, but Brynhild found that he was infirm of will and unsteady of thought. With Guttorm, then, she would work for the slaying of Sigurd. Her mind was fixed that he and she would no longer be in the world of men.

She made a dish of madness for Guttorm — serpent's venom and wolf's flesh mixed — and when he had eaten it Guttorm was crazed. Then did he listen to Brynhild's words. And she commanded him to go into the chamber where Sigurd slept and stab him through the body with a sword.

This Guttorm did. But Sigurd, before he gasped out his life, took Gram, his great sword, and flung it at Guttorm and cut him in twain.

And Brynhild, knowing what deed was done, went without and came to where Grani, Sigurd's proud horse, was standing. She stayed there with her arms across Grani's neck, the Valkyrie leaning across the horse that was born of Odin's horse. And Grani stood listening for some sound. He heard the cries of Gudrun over Sigurd, and then his heart burst and he died.

They bore Sigurd out of the Hall and Brynhild went beside where they placed him. She took a sword and put it through her own heart. Thus died Brynhild who had been made a mortal woman for her disobedience to the will of Odin, and who was won to be a mortal's wife by a falseness.

They took Sigurd and his horse Grani, and his helmet and his golden war-gear and they left all on a great painted ship. They could not but leave Brynhild beside him, Brynhild with her wondrous hair and her stern and beautiful face. They left the two together and launched the ship on the sea. And when the ship was on the water they fired it, and Brynhild once again lay in the flames.

And so Sigurd and Brynhild went together to join Baldur and Nanna in Hela's habitation.

Gunnar and Högni came to dread the evil that was in the hoard. They took the gleaming and glittering mass and they brought it to the river along which, ages before, Hreidmar had his smithy and the Dwarf Andvari his cave. From a rock in the river they cast the gold and jewels into the water and the hoard of Andvari sank for ever beneath the waves. Then the River Maidens had possession again of their treasure. But not for long were they to guard it and to sing over it, for now the season that was called the Fimbul Winter was coming over the earth, and Ragnarök, the Twilight of the Gods, was coming to the Dwellers in Asgard.

THE TWILIGHT OF THE GODS

SNOW fell on the four quarters of the world; icy winds blew from every side; the sun and the moon were hidden by storms. It was the Fimbul Winter: no spring came and no summer; no autumn brought harvest or fruit, and winter grew into winter again.

There was three years' winter. The first was called the Winter of Winds: storms blew and snows drove down and frosts were mighty. The children of men might hardly keep alive in that dread winter.

The second winter was called the Winter of the Sword: those who were left alive amongst men robbed and slew for what was left to feed on; brother fell on brother and slew him, and over all the world there were mighty battles.

And the third winter was called the Winter of the Wolf.

Then the ancient witch who lived in Jarnvid, the Iron Wood, fed the Wolf Managarm on unburied men and on the corpses of those who fell in battle. Mightily grew and flourished the Wolf that was to be the devourer of Mani, the Moon. The Champions in Valhalla would find their seats splashed with the blood that Managarm dashed from his jaws; this was a sign to the Gods that the time of the last battle was approaching.

A cock crew; far down in the bowels of the earth he was and beside Hela's habitation: the rusty-red cock of Hel crew, and his crowing made a stir in the lower worlds. In Jötunheim a cock crew, Fialar, the crimson cock, and at his crowing the Giants aroused themselves. High up in Asgard a cock crew, the golden cock Gullinkambir, and at his crowing the Champions in Valhalla bestirred themselves.

A dog barked; deep down in the earth a dog barked; it was Garm, the hound with bloody mouth, barking in Gnipa's Cave. The Dwarfs who heard groaned before their doors of stone. The tree Ygdrassil moaned in all its branches. There was a rending noise as the Giants moved their ship; there was a trampling sound as the hosts of Muspelheim gathered their horses.

But Jötunheim and Muspelheim and Hel waited tremblingly; it might be that Fenrir the Wolf might not burst the bonds wherewith the Gods had bound him. Without his being loosed the Gods might not be destroyed. And then was heard the rending of the rock as Fenrir broke loose. For the second time the Hound Garm barked in Gnipa's Cave.

Then was heard the galloping of the horses of the riders of Muspelheim; then was heard the laughter of Loki; then was heard the blowing of Heimdall's horn; then was heard the opening of Valhalla's five hundred and forty doors, as eight hundred Champions made ready to pass through each door.

Odin took council with Mimir's head. Up from the waters of the Well of Wisdom he drew it, and by the power of the runes he knew he made the head speak to him. Where best might the Æsir and the Vanir and the Einherjar, who were the Champions of Midgard, meet, and how best might they strive with the forces of Muspelheim and Jötunheim and Hel? The head of Mimir counseled Odin to meet them on Vigard Plain and to wage there such war that the powers of evil would be destroyed forever, even though his own world should be destroyed with them.

The riders of Muspelheim reached Bifröst, the Rainbow Bridge. Now would they storm the City of the Gods and fill it with flame. But Bifröst broke under the weight of the riders of Muspelheim, and they came not to the City of the Gods.

Jörmungand, the serpent that encircles the world, reared itself up from the sea. The waters flooded the lands, and the remnant of the world's inhabitants was swept away. That mighty flood floated Naglfar, the Ship of Nails that the Giants were so long building, and floated the ship of Hel also. With Hrymer the Giant steering it, Naglfar sailed against the Gods, with all the powers of Jötunheim aboard. And Loki steered the ship of Hel with the Wolf Fenrir upon it for the place of the last battle.

Since Bifröst was broken, the Æsir and the Vanir, the Asyniur and the Vana, the Einherjer and the Valkyries rode downward to Vigard through the waters of Thund. Odin rode at the head of his Champions. His helmet was of gold and in his hand was his spear Gungnir. Thor and Tyr were in his company.

In Mirkvid, the Dark Forest, the Vanir stood against the host of Muspelheim. From the broken end of the Rainbow Bridge the riders came, all flashing and flaming, with fire before them and after them. Niörd was there with Skadi, his Giant wife, fierce in her war-dress; Freya was there also, and Frey had Gerda beside him as a battle-maiden. Terribly bright flashed Surtur's sword. No sword ever owned was as bright as his except the sword that Frey had given to Skirnir. Frey and Surtur fought; he perished, Frey perished in that battle, but he would not have perished if he had had in his hand his own magic sword.

And now, for the third time, Garm, the hound with blood upon his jaws, barked. He had broken loose on the world, and with fierce bounds he rushed toward Vigard Plain, where the Gods had assembled their powers. Loud barked Garm. The Eagle Hræsvelgur screamed on the edge of heaven. Then the skies were cloven, and the tree Ygdrassil was shaken in all its roots.

To the place where the Gods had drawn up their ranks came the ship of Jötunheim and the ship of Hel, came the riders of Muspelheim, and Garm, the hound with blood upon his jaws. And out of the sea that now surrounded the plain of Vigard the serpent Jörmungand came.

What said Odin to the Gods and to the Champions who surrounded him? "We will give our lives and let our world be destroyed, but we will battle so that these evil powers will not live after us." Out of Hel's ship sprang Fenrir the Wolf. His mouth gaped; his lower jaw hung against the earth, and his upper jaw scraped the sky. Against the Wolf Odin All-Father fought. Thor might not aid him, for Thor had now to encounter Jörmungand, the monstrous serpent.

By Fenrir the Wolf Odin was slain. But the younger Gods were now advancing to the battle; and Vidar, the Silent God, came face to face with Fenrir. He laid his foot on the Wolf's lower jaw, that foot that had on the sandal made of all the scraps of leather that shoemakers had laid by for him, and with his hands he seized the upper jaw and tore his gullet. Thus died Fenrir, the fiercest of all the enemies of the Gods.

Jörmungand, the monstrous serpent, would have overwhelmed all with the venom he was ready to pour forth. But Thor sprang forward and crushed him with a stroke of his hammer Miölnir. Then Thor stepped back nine paces. But the serpent blew his venom over him, and blinded and choked and burnt, Thor, the World's Defender, perished.

Loki sprang from his ship and strove with Heimdall, the Warder of the Rainbow Bridge and the Watcher for the Gods. Loki slew Heimdall and was slain by him.

Bravely fought Tyr, the God who had sacrificed his swordhand for the binding of the Wolf. Bravely he fought, and many of the powers of evil perished by his strong left hand. But Garm, the hound with bloody jaws, slew Tyr.

And now the riders of Muspelheim came down on the field. Bright and gleaming were all their weapons. Before them and behind them went wasting fires. Surtur cast fire upon the earth; the tree Ygdrassil took fire and burned in all its great branches; the World Tree was wasted in the blaze. But the fearful fire that Surtur brought on the earth destroyed him and all his host.

The Wolf Hati caught up on Sol, the Sun; the Wolf Managarm seized on Mani, the Moon; they devoured them; stars fell, and darkness came down on the world.

The seas flowed over the burnt and wasted earth and the skies were dark above the sea, for Sol and Mani were no more. But at last the seas drew back and earth appeared again, green and beautiful. A new Sun and a new Moon appeared in the heavens, one a daughter of Sol and the other a daughter of Mani. No grim wolves kept them in pursuit.

Four of the younger Gods stood on the highest of the world's peaks; they were Vidar and Vali, the sons of Odin, and Modi and Magni, the sons of Thor. Modi and Magni found Miölnir, Thor's hammer, and with it they slew the monsters that still raged through the world, the Hound Garm and the Wolf Managarm.

Vidar and Vali found in the grass the golden tablets on which were inscribed the runes of wisdom of the elder

Gods. The runes told them of a heaven that was above Asgard, of Gimli, that was untouched by Surtur's fire. Vili and Ve, Will and Holiness, ruled in it. Baldur and Hödur came from Hela's habitation, and the Gods sat on the peak together and held speech with each other, calling to mind the secrets and the happenings they had known before Ragnarök, the Twilight of the Gods.

Deep in a wood two of human kind were left; the fire of Surtur did not touch them; they slept, and when they wakened the world was green and beautiful again. These two fed on the dews of the morning; a woman and a man they were, Lif and Lifthrasir. They walked abroad in the world, and from them and from their children came the men and women who spread themselves over the earth.